Measuring Treatment Progress

DATE DUE

Measuring Treatment Progress

AN OUTCOME STUDY GUIDEBOOK

Patricia L. Owen, Ph.D.

HAZELDEN®

Hazelden
Center City, Minnesota 55012-0176

1-800-328-0094
1-651-213-4590 (Fax)
www.hazelden.org

Library of Congress Cataloging-in-Publication Data

Owen, Patricia, 1951–
    Measuring treatment progress : an outcome study guidebook /
    Patricia L. Owen.
        p. cm.
    Includes bibliographical references and index.
    ISBN 1-56838-982-5 (paperback)
    1. Addicts—Rehabilitation—Evaluation. 2. Substance abuse—
Treatment—Evaluation. 3. Drug abuse—Treatment—Evaluation.
4. Substance abuse—Patients—Rehabilitation—Evaluation.
5. Drug abuse—Patients—Rehabilitation—Evaluation.
6. Outcome assessment (Medical care)—Methodology. I. Title.

RC564.O945 2003
616.86'03—dc21   2002191908

07 06 05 04 03   6 5 4 3 2 1

Cover design by David Spohn
Interior design and typesetting by Kinne Design

Contents

Illustrations

Acknowledgments

Special thanks go to Dee Reilly who has maintained Hazelden's outcome monitoring systems over the years and supervises a wonderful staff of interviewers, including Betty Benjamin, Ann Gartman, Judy Priebe, and Marjorie Stucky. Thanks, too, to Valerie Slaymaker, Ph.D., for her development of special outcome studies and to Debbie Anthony for her help in holding together all we do. And, of course, deep gratitude goes to all the patients over the years who have participated in outcome studies, giving Hazelden the continued information upon which to grow and improve.

Introduction

Addiction to alcohol and other drugs has caused, and continues to cause, untold problems for individuals, for their families, and for our society. Hazelden not only has pioneered in developing treatment programs to help people who suffer from the disease of addiction but also it leads in refining and improving treatment approaches. As part of this effort, Hazelden conducts thorough outcome studies to answer the question, Does treatment work? Outcome studies aim at gaining a more thorough understanding of how often treatment works and what about it works for whom. These difficult questions must be answered if we want to improve the programs we offer for this devastating disease.

Two kinds of studies form "bookends" for the field of outcome studies: naturalistic and empirical. One type of study is not better than the other. Rather, empirical and naturalistic studies give two different and valuable perspectives.

Naturalistic studies, the type most frequently used by treatment programs, examine programs as they exist and the patients participating in them. These studies do not try to control variables. Rather, they are "real-world" studies of people who go to treatment and their outcomes.

Empirical studies, also known as treatment efficacy studies, test how well a specific treatment performs for certain patients. In these studies, participants are as homogeneous as possible in background and in alcohol- and drug-use characteristics. Standardized instruments are used to gather information, and subjects are randomly assigned to groups. In other words, all of the variables are tightly controlled.

Because variables are controlled, empirical studies allow researchers to be fairly sure that observed changes are due to the treatment being applied. Naturalistic studies, sometimes called effectiveness studies, are "messier" because it's hard to pin down the sources or reasons for apparent change. At the same time, they may also provide a more realistic picture of treatment than do empirical studies.

Conducting studies that meet the rigorous scientific standards of empirical research requires considerable effort and goes beyond the scope of *Measuring Treatment Progress*. What you will find in this book is a simple, straightforward guide to doing a naturalistic outcome study. *Measuring Treatment Progress* will also show you how to present your results to patients and others in a way that is logical and easy to understand. And, finally, this book will give you information on unique populations and settings, an overview of significant recent studies, and a host of resources to help you design and customize each new study to meet the specific needs of your stakeholders.

$\succ$

1

Planning Your Outcome Study

"Our treatment center's one year anniversary is coming up, and we want to pull together an outcome study on our patients. How do we do that?"

• • •

"I want to prove to the companies that refer their employees to us that treatment is worth it, that it saves their company money."

• • •

"We want to know whether our short-stay program is as effective as our traditional program with a longer length of stay."

• • •

"We provide alcohol and drug services within our HMO and want to examine whether our programs are cost-effective for the overall plan."

In today's complex world of increasing requests for human services on the one hand and diminishing resources on the other, there is a growing demand for solid information about what works and what doesn't. This is as true in the field of addiction treatment as it is in any other human services field. More than ever before, payers, family members, and program administrators want to know if treatment really works. This is a hard question to answer, given the multitude of variables involved. It's also an important question. If providing the answer is your job, you will want to make sure your answer is as accurate and complete as possible.

Fortunately, as the demand for outcome information has grown, so has the ability to provide reliable, multifaceted information. *Measuring Treatment Progress* will help you give timely and accurate outcome information to people inquiring if your treatment program works. It looks at the multitude of things to consider as you design a naturalistic outcome study—a real-world study conducted on a treatment program, as it exists using its current participants as the study sample. The book includes chapters on initial planning, selecting an information-gathering method, choosing or designing research tools, analyzing the data, and writing the report. There are additional chapters on studying outcomes in special populations or treatment settings, an overview of some landmark studies you may find instructive as you design and conduct your studies, and an exploration of new directions in the field.

Initial Planning

Many considerations go into developing an outcome study. These range from understanding the program goals to deciding exactly who should be included in the study and how to approach them. Constructing your study can be as elementary as building a flower box or as complex as building a mansion. However, no matter what level of study you are building, there are three basic questions to answer in the initial planning stage:

- Who wants to know the outcomes?
- What do they want to know?
- When do they want to know it?

Answering these questions as thoroughly as possible right from the beginning will help you produce a report that gives everyone the information they want and need. Let's take a closer look at each of these.

Who Wants to Know the Outcomes?

Several types of groups, or stakeholders, may be interested in the information your outcome study will generate. It's important to identify these groups or individuals because each of them may want different information. Interested parties can range from people inside the organization to vaguely defined groups outside the organization and to specific groups or individuals. Stakeholders typically include licensing and accreditation bodies, payers, referring organizations, prospective patients and their families, your organization's board members, your organization's administrators, and clinicians.

Take time to think about who will be looking at this study. Who often calls and asks, "Do you have any outcome data on Program X?" Make a list of individuals and groups that you know will want the data or that you'd like to receive the information. Identifying each stakeholder group ahead of time helps ensure that you will not miss important components in your design.

What Do They Want to Know?

Let's look at each main stakeholder group and examine what type of questions they are most likely to have about outcomes.

LICENSING AND ACCREDITATION BODIES want to know that the program is well run and methodical in how it evaluates its performance. Their typical questions include

- How does your organization measure its performance?
- Why have you taken this approach?
- How do program administrators and staff use outcome data to make improvements?

The primary accreditation body for treatment programs is the Joint Commission on Accreditation of Healthcare Organizations (JCAHO). JCAHO requires two things of all health care providers seeking or wanting to maintain JCAHO accreditation. First, it requires that an organization collect and use information about its process and outcomes to improve services. Second, JCAHO requires providers to collect certain outcome indicators and report them on an ongoing basis. JCAHO calls this second, relatively new requirement its "ORYX initiative." More information about the ORYX initiative can be obtained at www.jcaho.org. Because JCAHO requires that providers use certain approved standardized indicators, most providers will contract with a measurement vendor that has already received approval from JCAHO for its specific measures.

PAYERS want to know if the treatment program is worth the money they are investing in it. Employers and holders of company contracts may ask, "Do employees return from treatment as 'good workers'?" In other words, do they come to work on time, have good attendance, demonstrate safe conduct, and maintain good working relationships with supervisors and coworkers? Insurers and other health care funders may ask, "Does the program produce good results at the same or less cost than other methods of providing care? Are the services, including length of stay and modalities, individualized to produce the maximum outcome for the least cost?"

REFERRING ORGANIZATIONS want to know if they made a good decision sending you their clients. Typical questions include

- How well do you do with a specific type of client, such as a person who has depression or a member of a certain social class or racial group?
- What percentage of people are abstinent and have an improved quality of life, an improved mental health functioning, and better family relationships?
- Do clients have a specific and realistic continuing care plan?

PROSPECTIVE PATIENTS AND THEIR FAMILIES want to know whether treatment will have a significant impact on the patient's life. Typical questions include

- What's the likelihood of success for someone like my loved one or for me (that is, someone of this age, with this type of drug use, with this number of previous treatments, with this dual disorder)?
- What can I do to maximize success? Does a longer stay in a halfway house after treatment increase likelihood of success?

BOARD MEMBERS OF THE TREATING ORGANIZATION have questions surrounding the overall quality of the organization. These questions might include

- What percentage of clients succeed in our program?
- Are clients and other stakeholders happy with the services they receive?
- What can we learn from other programs?
- Are our outcomes improving over time?

ADMINISTRATORS OF THE TREATMENT PROGRAM primarily want to know if the program has good results. Typical questions include

- Are our results consistently good?
- Are some programs performing better than others within our system, and, if so, can we generalize from this information?
- Are some programs not performing well? Why?

CLINICIANS want to know if they are making a difference in clients' lives. They ask questions such as

- What percentage are sober? Are their alcohol or drug problems less severe?

7

- What percentage have an improved overall life?
- Are they using what we taught them?

The best way to find out what your audience wants to know is to ask them. Interview one to two representatives of each stakeholder group or bring several together for a focus group. Tell them whether you are starting an outcome program or revising one. Ask for their input. You may wish to ask what outcomes are important to them, what they want to know about outcomes, and what questions they have about your treatment and its effectiveness. Asking your stakeholders for their input from the beginning of the project will help you refine your efforts and obtain overall cooperation in the process.

When Do They Want the Information?

There are three potential timelines for an outcome study: retrospective; periodic; and ongoing or rolling. The type you select often depends on the resources available and the purpose of the outcome study. Let's look at each of these timelines.

Retrospective Outcome Studies

Retrospective studies are useful if resources are limited or program administrators want information to help decide whether to continue a program. For this type of study, all program participants during a certain previous window of time, such as one year ago, are contacted. Data are collected and reported only on this specific group. If the program is small, the window may need to be expanded to obtain a reasonable sample size. Generally, a sample size of at least thirty clients is needed; a sample of sixty to one hundred patients is better. (See chapter 3 for a discussion of sample size.)

The advantage of a retrospective study is that it can be done relatively quickly. It also provides the opportunity for feedback even when an outcome study had not been planned at the outset of a program.

There are three disadvantages to retrospective studies. First, because they are done retrospectively, baseline data may not be available or may be inconsistent across time. For example, if you were not planning to follow up with these clients at one year, you may not have collected consistent information at the beginning of treatment about their alcohol or drug use and the consequences. Even if the information is available in narrative form in individual patient charts, the details may be uneven. In either case, you will not be able to compare patients' functioning at outcome with their functioning at the outset of treatment.

The second disadvantage is the likelihood of poor response rates. It may be difficult to locate clients if you have had no contact with them since treatment. Even if you are successful in locating them, they may not be willing participants for a program to which they no longer feel connected or for an evaluation project that they were not informed about when they were in treatment. It's best, if possible, to tell clients about the outcome study while they are in the program and encourage their participation after they leave the program.

A third disadvantage is the difficulty of getting permission from clients to include them in a retrospective outcome study. If you are gathering information for more than program use only, you may be legally required to obtain formal patient consent. If your program is a federally funded one, you must get formal prior patient consent. In other cases, you may be able to obtain the permission by phone at time of follow-up. Again, it's best if you can obtain clients' permission to contact them later while they are still in treatment.

Periodic Outcome Studies

Most outcome systems are maintained over time, producing annual reports based on the calendar year. Once the outcome monitoring system is established, all patients are contacted at consistent time intervals, and data are held and aggregated for reporting at the end of the year. This type of timeline has the advantage of allowing stakeholders to know when outcome data will be available.

The disadvantage is long time lags between data collection and reporting. For example, if you plan to do a one-year outcome study looking at all patients treated in 2003, the actual report will not be ready until early 2005. This is because the last one-year follow-up will be collected in December 2004 (or even January 2005), and one to three months are needed after that to aggregate the data and write the report. Understandably, stakeholders may be impatient with the timeline and discouraged that the results are relatively out-of-date when they do arrive.

Ongoing or Rolling Outcome Studies

If a program has adequate resources, reports can be generated for all patients treated during a set time as they emerge from treatment. These results can be displayed as columns of percentages that show changes or trends over time. For better visual display, the results also may be shown in a line graph.

As seen in figure 1.1 on page 11, outcomes are reported each month on all patients discharged two months previously. In this case, there is always a two-month time lag, which includes the month after treatment and another month to aggregate the information and prepare the report. The post-treatment time interval can be any length, and outcomes can be reported on all patients discharged twelve months previously.

The advantage to rolling reports is that they provide information on patients who have been recently treated. This is sometimes called "real-time" data, as the information can be acted on very soon after the event or treatment period, and not after a long delay. Trends can be easily spotted.

FIGURE 1.1
Rolling One-Month Outcome Results

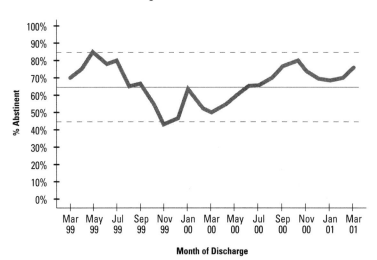

Month of Discharge

The disadvantage is that rolling reports produce many data points of small sample sizes rather than one report with a large sample size. Some stakeholders will be more comfortable with large sample sizes. A solution to this problem is that all data during the previous year can also be aggregated and reported in a more traditional annual report format.

Once you've answered the three main questions about who your stakeholders are, what they want to know, and how frequently they want reports, you are ready to begin designing your outcome monitoring system.

2

Deciding What to Measure

After you have answered the basic questions of who wants the information your study will provide, what kinds of information they want, and when, you must refine the nature of the outcome information. This involves articulating the goals of the program and defining program success, and then selecting the variables to measure that success.

Keeping It Simple

The biggest challenge in designing an outcome measurement system is to keep it simple enough to improve chances for success and, at the same time, detailed enough to capture the information that key stakeholders need. This balance is hard to achieve. It is difficult to refrain from devising an overly long list of questions because stakeholders typically have wide and varied interests. There is also an ubiquitous temptation to add a few more variables "as long as we are contacting clients anyway." Be careful about giving in to this temptation. It is important to keep the questionnaire simple for two reasons. First, if it is too long or complex, patients may be less willing to complete it or may not sustain good attention and accuracy. Second, once all the data are collected, it's easy to get bogged down with extraneous information when the main goal is to produce timely and useable reports.

Keeping questionnaires relatively short is difficult in designing any outcome system and particularly hard when measuring outcomes for the addiction field. This is because, first, addiction treatment is multifaceted and outcome measures must reflect this complexity; and, second, since no standardized approach exists, an array of variables must be used to allow comparison of outcomes from one study to another. While you want to keep the questionnaire short, you also need to ensure that you gather enough information to be useful.

Later in this chapter, we will look at nine categories of outcome variables that are essential to address in evaluating treatment success. You will generally want to measure some items from each category. However, as you develop the specific items for your questionnaire, think about what is critically needed to report basic outcomes on an ongoing basis. Asking a core set of questions on critical factors is far better than designing a long questionnaire about everything anyone may want to know.

Selecting Outcome Indicators

Your first task in designing a questionnaire is deciding exactly what to measure. In other words, you must decide what indicates that treatment was a success. This "what" is called an *outcome indicator*. It is also known as a *measurement variable*, that is, the variable (or variables) used to measure the degree of success.

Defining Success

There is a debate in the addiction field about what constitutes success and, therefore, what outcome indicators or variables should be measured in a study. Most programs hold the philosophy that success is measured by improvements across the multiple problems entangled with addiction. However, detractors ask if it is "fair" to expect treatment to resolve all the problems that alcohol and drug users bring to treatment.

Let's illustrate this debate with a hypothetical patient. Imagine a woman who meets diagnostic criteria for cocaine dependency and alcohol abuse. She is depressed and was recently hospitalized for a serious suicide attempt. She has a history of eating disorders, is significantly underweight, and has had numerous medical consequences as a result. She has missed many days of work and her job is in jeopardy. In addition, she is a single parent who hopes to regain custody of her two young children by completing treatment and maintaining sobriety. One side of the debate holds that treatment can only be considered successful for this patient if she shows improvement across the breadth of her problems. The other side holds that her treatment should be considered a success if she stops using alcohol or drugs. The latter argues that a patient with diabetes, or even depression, may have multiple problems, but treatment success is still measured by whether the diabetes is controlled, or whether the depression is resolved, and that alcohol or drug treatment should also be measured on similar terms.

The difficulty is that addicts' problems are rarely limited to just excessive use of a particular substance. Unlike diabetes, or even depression, the attendant problems in addicts' lives are intrinsic to the disease. Addicts are likely to use multiple substances at various levels of dependency or abuse and have many other life problems that contribute to or are caused by the dependency. Because patients come to treatment with multiple needs, treatment is typically multidimensional and cannot be adequately measured unless all these dimensions are addressed. Therefore, this book, consistent with most treatment programs, holds that a wide range of variables— from level of use to overall quality of life—is needed to measure the success of alcohol and drug treatment.

This position doesn't mean that an outcome study should never limit the scope of the variables to alcohol or drug use. You may measure primarily substance use if you are doing an outcome study limited to a factor such as the effect of a medication on substance use. However, most outcome studies of alcohol or drug use take the philosophy that dependency and its treatment are inherently complex, and, therefore, outcome measurement must reflect that complexity. In most outcome studies, the basic categories of outcome indicators include alcohol and drug use, treatment and recovery history, mental health, quality of life and relationships, employment, education, legal situation, health, and spiritual life. Before taking a closer look at these nine categories, the variables that can be used to measure them, and appropriate questions to assess them, let's talk a little more about the complexity of choosing variables to measure success in addiction treatment.

Measuring Treatment Goals

What you choose to measure will be influenced, in part, by the goal of the treatment program you are assessing. For example, many methadone maintenance programs are most concerned with decreased use of heroin, decreased arrests, and decreased jail time. Employee assistance programs may be most concerned with job-performance indicators. Table 2.1 on page 17 shows various types of treatment programs and examples of variables that would typically be areas of inquiry.

While a specific program's goals will influence the outcome indicators selected, it's also important to use measures that can be "translated" across treatment types so that comparisons can be made. For example, even if your program goal is total abstinence, it would also be helpful to measure other, more detailed alcohol- or drug-use variables, such as number of times the person drank or used in the follow-up period. Similarly, programs that are most interested in reduced use should also measure overall abstinence. This way, when the results are reported, each program will be able to understand what the other's outcomes are. While researchers may focus on one type of program or setting, the disease is the same across settings, and many patients find themselves in a number of them over the course of their lives.

TABLE 2.1

Relationship between Program Type and Outcome Measures

TYPE	GOAL	MEASURES
Medications	Decreased use	Craving Days to first use Amount of use per day Number of days used Side effects
Corrections	Decreased criminal behavior and recidivism	*In prison:* Level of cooperation Number of disciplinary offenses *After release from prison:* Days to first use Days to first arrest Days to first conviction Days to first incarceration
Health services	Improved overall health and reduced health services	Comparison of health care services used before and after treatment
Work-oriented treatment program program or EAP* *Employee Assistance Program	Improved productivity	Absenteeism Job performance Job attitude and behavior Workers' compensation costs
Women- or family-oriented program	Self-sufficiency	Job acquisition Job retention Progress toward financial self-sufficiency Parenting skills Regaining or maintaining custody of children
Harm reduction program	Decreased use and decreased societal problems due to use	Amount of use per day Number of days used Number of heavy drinking days
Twelve Step program	Recovery; abstinence and a better overall life	Number of AA meetings attended Use of sponsor Number of Steps worked Use of Big Book, other reading Spiritual growth or fitness Abstinence Adherence to continuing care recommendations Quality of life

Defining Variables

As you select the variables to use in measuring success, you will also need to define those variables. For instance, most studies agree that abstinence is one of the outcome indicators to measure. However, even the seemingly simple concept of "abstinence" is measured in a myriad of ways and varies by length of time, strictness of definition of "abstinence," types of substances included, and the method of measurement. Table 2.2 shows the different ways abstinence is measured in various published research studies.

Table 2.2 shows that one of the abstinence definitions includes "one lapse." Some researchers have even included in their measures an allowance for the idea that people may relapse more than once, but get back on track and do well. Some researchers also look at various levels of drinking after treatment. These are controversial categories for programs

TABLE 2.2

Measurement of Abstinence

	ABSTINENCE OR USE MEASURES
Length of time	Full follow-up period since treatment
	Last 30, 60, or 90 days prior to follow-up contact
Strictness of definition	Continuous abstinence (no use)
	Continuous abstinence with one "lapse"
	Percent of drinking (using) days
	Average number of drinks per drinking day
	(Use of a mood-altering medication may not disqualify participant as abstinent if medication was prescribed and used as prescribed.)
Types of substances	May pertain to all categories of alcohol and drugs
	May pertain only to alcohol, or the target drug treated
How measured	Self-report
	Urinalysis/blood test

whose goal is total abstinence. However, lumping together all patients who return to any level of drinking as treatment failures may underestimate treatment effectiveness. Consider the example of treatment outcome indicators developed by researchers[1] using data from the large-scale national study called Project MATCH, shown in table 2.3. (See chapter 7 for more information about Project MATCH.)

TABLE 2.3
Composite Measure of Abstinence

	FEMALES	MALES
Abstinent	No drinking during the 3 months prior to follow-up contact	No drinking during the 3 months prior to follow-up contact
Moderate Drinking	Fewer than 4 drinks per day of drinking and fewer than 12 drinks per week of drinking OR no more than 2 occasions of 4 or more drinks per day of drinking and 12 or more drinks per week of drinking	Fewer than 6 drinks per day of drinking and fewer than 15 drinks per week of drinking OR no more than 2 occasions of 6 or more drinks per day of drinking and 15 or more drinks per week of drinking
Heavy Drinking	Three or more occasions of 4 or more drinks per day of drinking and 12 or more drinks per week of drinking	Three or more occasions of 6 or more drinks per day of drinking and 15 or more drinks per week of drinking

In addition, these researchers developed criteria for different levels of alcohol-related problems, enabling them to classify people as *abstinent, moderate drinker,* or *heavy drinker* "with problems" or "without problems." Grouping people into these categories enabled researchers to capture more of the complexity in drinking patterns and consequences at outcomes. In this case, they found that at one-year outcome, 37 percent were abstinent, 10 percent were drinking moderately without problems, 14 percent were drinking moderately with problems or drinking heavily without problems, and

39 percent were drinking heavily with problems. This breakdown is more informative than the purely dichotomous information that 37 percent were abstinent and 63 percent had used alcohol. (Note that in this study "abstinence" was measured as no alcohol in the past ninety days.)

Basic Categories of Outcome Indicators

As we have seen, there are many complications to consider as you choose what to measure, including the multifaceted aspects of treatment, the goals or orientation of the treatment program, how you define success, and how you define the specific variables to measure success. Still, there are certain basic categories of outcome indicators to address as you design your questionnaire, as well as certain variables that are generally used to measure success in each category. These categories and variables include

- Alcohol and drug use: quantity and frequency of use; alcohol-/drug-use diagnoses.
- Treatment and recovery history: number of previous treatments; participation in self-help groups; length of longest abstinence.
- Mental health: history of psychiatric problems; current diagnoses; medications; current level of functioning/symptoms.
- Quality of life and relationships: stability of relationships; type of social network (using or abstinent/in recovery); amount of social involvement and support; patients' overall rating of their own quality of life.
- Employment: stability of employment; ability to work; consistent, adequate performance.
- Education (especially for youth): attainment commensurate with developmental stage; consistent, adequate performance; suspensions or expulsions.

- Legal situation: number of legal problems.
- Health: overall level of health; use of medical services.
- Spiritual life: stability and satisfaction with relationship to a Higher Power.

In addition, certain basic information needs to be collected at intake (or time of treatment). This includes demographic information, specifically, age, gender, race/ethnicity, and educational level. You should also collect information on age of first use of alcohol or drugs and age of first problem.

Keeping in mind that these nine categories of outcome indicators are basic to measuring the success of most treatment programs, and keeping in mind the need to strike a balance between simplicity and thoroughness, we will now move on to discuss questions you can use to glean information.

$$\succ$$

3

Designing the Questionnaire

Once you have sorted through the complexities of defining what constitutes the success you want to measure and what variables will allow you to do so, the next step is to develop a questionnaire, or tool, that will let you do a good job. In this chapter, we will look at the variety of questionnaires available, how you might customize them, and how to test the questionnaire you finally settle on.

Choosing Measurement Tools

The best—and easiest—method for measuring success is to use standardized questionnaires. Standardized questionnaires have already undergone use and statistical analysis to determine whether the items have sufficient reliability and validity. Reliability means the items yield consistent information. Validity means the survey measures what it purports to measure. Standardized instruments may also have norms, which allow you to compare your results with the results of other studies. Last but not least, the work of developing the questions has already been done for you.

Note that full-scale questionnaire development, with sound psychometric properties, is beyond the scope of this book. If you do reach a point where you want to design a questionnaire to measure a specific construct, or content area such as spirituality or recovery or well-being, it is important to understand and use appropriate statistical methods. See the sidebar Constructing a Test on page 24 for a brief overview of what is needed to develop a psychometrically sound measurement instrument. The main point, for our purposes, is that full-scale test development requires more resources and a different set of skills than may be available. This is yet another reason why using already-established scales and instruments is often the best way to go.

CONSTRUCTING A TEST

To develop a psychometrically sound outcome measurement instrument, the following steps should be followed:

1. Obtain the items through literature reviews, expert interviews, and experience with the patient population.
2. Form questions and responses.
3. Do a factor analysis to determine the main factor or factors and eliminate items that do not contribute much to the overall scale or scales.
4. Evaluate internal consistency of each scale to determine how well the items hang together (a form of reliability).
5. Examine a different form of consistency, over time, by giving the scale or scales to the same group of people over two short periods. For most scales, you will expect to see consistent responses at both points in time.
6. Examine the validity of the scale or scales, that is, whether the scale is measuring what you intend it to measure. Validity can typically be established in two ways. First, concurrent validity can be examined by comparing your new scale with something similar already established or available in the environment. For example, if you built a scale that purportedly measures an individual's progress in recovery, you would expect to see some congruence between an individual's scale score and ratings on similar items by a counselor or other close observer. A second way to measure validity is to look at how well the scale predicts future behavior. This is called predictive validity. Using the same scale measuring progress in recovery, you would expect that favorable scores on this scale would correlate highly with abstinence at a later point in time.
7. Finally, you will look at average, range, and variability of scores across different population groups to establish norms.

More detailed information on the process of test construction can be obtained from most basic statistical or research textbooks.

Study Sample

Let's digress here for a moment to mention study sample, or the participants in the study you are conducting. Naturalistic studies allow little control over the study sample. Sampling in a naturalistic study is known as a "convenience sample" since everyone available is included and not just patients who have particular characteristics or who have received specific treatment approaches. Convenience sampling makes naturalistic studies less rigorous than empirical studies. On the other hand, the results may have more real-world applicability in that people have not been artificially excluded on the basis of severity, dual disorder, or drug type. Because you cannot ensure a homogeneous sample, it is more difficult to determine if patients' successes or failures are due to treatment or to their very different histories. You can still get an abundance of useful information; however, it will be important to establish a certain sample size to increase the validity of the information. In fact, if you know you want to look at particular subgroups, for example, by gender, age, or type of drug, you will need to make sure you have large enough subgroups to analyze. A good rule of thumb is to strive for at least thirty in any subgroup.

Comprehensive Standardized Questionnaires

When selecting a questionnaire, you may wish first to consider comprehensive standardized instruments that include almost all the core items you will need. This is the simplest approach to developing your questionnaire. These instruments include the Addiction Severity Index (ASI) and a combination of Form 90 and the Drinker Inventory of Consequences (DrInC).

Addiction Severity Index (ASI)

The Addiction Severity Index was developed by Thomas McLellan and his colleagues in 1980 as a standardized method to obtain information about a patient's alcohol and drug use and several aspects of the patient's life.[1] It has undergone several revisions and is now in its fifth edition.[2] The ASI is a structured interview, about one hour in length. The domains measured are medical status, employment/support status, alcohol use, drug use, legal status, family/social relationships, and psychiatric status. Scoring for each of the seven domains yields a composite score on a scale from 0 to 1, with the latter being the most severe. The fifth edition of the ASI is provided in appendix 2.

Advantages of the ASI include being well-known, well-regarded, and much-used, particularly in research. This means there are ample published studies for comparison purposes. The ASI covers most of the critical life domains affected by alcohol and drug use. Because separate scores are given for each domain, there is good intuitive appeal to the results. The items are detailed, clear, and easily understood by the respondent. In addition, an abbreviated form of the ASI can be given at follow-up intervals so that changes in severity can be documented. Work is in progress to design a self-administered version of the ASI.

The ASI has disadvantages. Staff using this instrument need to receive training on administration and scoring. Ideally, the ASI becomes a routine part of intake and assessment, administered by clinical staff in lieu of routine program measures or more informal interviews. However, some staff or programs may be unwilling to give up their current method of assessment for the ASI. In this case, the ASI will need to be administered separately by outcome evaluation staff.

Another drawback is that the time frame for ASI questions is very recent—a snapshot of the thirty days prior to the interview. This means that continuous or overall level of use since treatment will not be captured. Another thing to consider is that, while the interview contains many items, the domain scores are based on relatively few items. For example, alcohol severity is measured only on a composite of days of alcohol use, days of alcohol intoxication, how patients respond to questions about being "troubled" or "bothered" by alcohol problems, how important treatment for alcohol problems is to them now, and how much money they have spent on alcohol. Other potentially important factors, such as length of use and consequences of use, are not included in this scale. Scoring includes computing log values, which may not be a familiar mathematical method for staff. Finally, the ASI is not standardized across the seven subscales. In other words, a score of .80 on the psychiatric subscale and a score of .20 on the legal subscale does not necessarily mean a person has greater psychiatric problems than legal problems.

Information about the ASI is available online at the Web site of its developers, the Treatment Research Institute (TRI): www.densonline.org/ASICT.pdf. This site includes the full ASI and scoring information. TRI is involved in a major project using the ASI called the Drug Evaluation Network System, or DENS. Information about DENS is also available at this site. A document regarding use of the ASI with Native American populations is available from the Center for Substance Abuse Treatment (CSAT) at www.treatment.org/documents/chapter1_3.pdf.

Form 90 and the Drinker Inventory of Consequences (DrInC)
Form 90 and the Drinker Inventory of Consequences, spawned by the major research study Project MATCH, have a strong history of standardization and acceptance in the field.[3] Form 90 is a structured interview based on Linda Sobell's timeline followback methodology.[4] It uses a calendar and cues to help an individual recreate the quantity and frequency of alcohol use over a previous period. Generally, the questions ask about the previous ninety days (hence the name of the instrument), but other time periods can be used. Many versions of Form 90

have been created: versions for in-person or telephone interviews, a long form and a short form, versions for patients or collateral informants, and versions for drug use. The full version includes methods to collect information about days of incarceration, treatment, medical services, medications, work, education, and other life activities. The Form 90 manual, designed as part of Project MATCH, contains all the versions and instructions for their use. It is available from the U.S. government and can be ordered online at www.niaaa.nig.gov/publications/match.htm or by using the order form provided in appendix 1. The short version appears in appendix 3.

The DrInC is a fifty-item paper-and-pencil questionnaire that covers consequences of alcohol use. It consists of five subscales: physical consequences, intrapersonal consequences, social responsibility consequences, interpersonal consequences, and impulse control consequences. As with Form 90, there are many versions of this scale, including a short form, a form for collateral reporting, and a form for drugs as well as alcohol. The manual for the DrInC can also be ordered through the National Institute of Alcohol Abuse and Alcoholism (NIAAA) at www.niaaa.nih.gov/publications/match.htm. An order form for the DrInC is also provided in appendix 1.

Form 90 and the DrInC combined provide a comprehensive assessment of a person's alcohol and drug use and related consequences. They are psychometrically sound and have enough flexibility to suit the data collection needs of most researchers.

The biggest disadvantage is the DrInC's focus on consequences that the respondent specifically attributes to alcohol or drug use. For example, in the alcohol version, all items include the phrase ". . . because of my drinking." Representative items include "I have lost a marriage or a close love relationship because of my drinking," "I have lost a friend because of my drinking," and "I have lost interest in activities and hobbies because of my drinking." This frame of reference produces two potential problems. First, at baseline, some people may recognize problems in their lives but may not readily associate these problems with their alcohol or drug use. Second, at follow-up, the items are not applicable to respondents who are abstinent. While at that point the items could be asked without the phrase ". . . because of my drinking" to obtain a more general picture of a person's quality of life, the comparability to baseline data is lost. The best solution may be to add a separate, brief measure of general quality of life at baseline and follow up for a measure of overall life functioning.

Other Questionnaires and "Borrowed" Questions

Instead of using an established, complete battery of instruments, you may wish to "mix and match" sections of questionnaires or add questionnaires that are aimed at specific categories. While you will need to guard against compromising the psychometric integrity of an already-standardized instrument, the advantage of a mix-and-match approach is that you may end up with a questionnaire that is more relevant to the specific outcomes you are trying to measure.

You may also wish to add some specialized questions or questionnaires to do special, time-limited studies while continuing to do a comprehensive outcome study. For example, you may decide to do a more in-depth study on spirituality, or Alcoholics Anonymous (AA) involvement, or mental health issues. You can add focused key questions on your topic for the time-limited study. Then, after completing that special study, you may wish to implement another study, perhaps on return-to-work factors, family relationships, or the role of recreation in recovery. At that point, you can drop the first special-topic questions and add the new ones to the core items.

If you decide, when you mix and match, to use only portions of standardized instruments, be sure to select sections that have "stand-alone" validity and reliability in order to maintain the instrument's psychometric integrity. For example, with the DrInC, it would be better to use the already-established short form than to "handpick" items from the long form. Likewise, with Form 90, it would be better to use the recommended short version than to edit the standard longer instrument. If possible, add unique or unstandardized questions after the instruments with established reliability and validity. That way, there is less likelihood of "contaminating" the standardized instrument.

Some standardized instruments that can be mixed and matched to address the various categories of outcome indicators are reviewed below, as are questions developed by Hazelden to address the categories.

Alcohol and Drug Use

In addition to quantity and frequency items incorporated into Form 90, the ASI, or other standardized instruments, it is sometimes helpful to ask more general questions regarding alcohol or drug use. The results can be used to augment or explain more specific alcohol- or drug-use items. Hazelden surveys have found the following general questions to be useful:

GENERAL USE QUESTION

If time allows, ask the question below separately for alcohol and for other drugs. It is intended to be a follow-up item after more specific items about quantity and frequency of drug use and can be helpful for getting an overall picture from the patient's point of view and/or fill in time gaps between interview window and time since treatment.

> Overall, how would you describe your alcohol and
> drug use since treatment *(years, months)* ago?

_____ (1) totally abstinent

_____ (2) used for a period of time, then stopped
and have remained abstinent

_____ (3) off-and-on periods of use and abstinence

_____ (4) more or less continuous use

PERCEPTION OF PROBLEM AND ACTION QUESTION

In very short questionnaires, especially if Form 90 or a comparable tool is not used, it is sometimes difficult to capture the pattern of use. Inevitably, stakeholders will wonder whether people who relapse are able to return to abstinence or continue to use.

(If used) Has your use caused any problems?

_____ (1) Yes, and I quit or sought help.

_____ (2) Yes, but I continue to use.

_____ (3) No, no problems.

For this item in particular, keep in mind that the responses are based on self-report. When questions are general and subjective, they are more open to interpretation, and it is more likely you will get inaccurate or inconsistent information. On the other hand, while specific and factual questions will yield more accurate information, they may not give the "big picture." For example, if you want to know whether a person's alcohol or drug use after treatment is problematic, you may simply ask directly: "Did your use cause problems?" Alternatively, you could ask, "On a scale from 0 to 5, where 0 is 'no problems' and 5 is 'extreme problems,' how much of a problem, if any, did your use cause?" Because these questions are subjective and relatively nonspecific, you will get a myriad of responses that are difficult to interpret. What one person considers a problem may not be considered a problem by another. For instance, one person may not consider getting a citation for drunk driving a problem while another may consider forgetting a promise a major problem. The solution is to depend more on factual information, such as asking respondents about specific behaviors or consequences (number of driving infractions, number of days missed at work, etc.). If you include items that are diagnostic criteria for substance abuse, you will get both detailed information about types of problems associated with use, as well as what percentage are using at levels that professionals would consider problematic, such as meeting criteria for abuse or dependence. Criteria for substance abuse and dependence are found in the American Psychiatric Association's *Diagnostic and Statistical Manual of Mental Disorders*, or *DSM-IV*.[5]

A person may believe his or her continued use is not a problem, but facts may be different. If you have both the respondent's subjective point of view and factual information, it is possible to make a statement such as: "Of those who used after treatment, 40 percent returned to abstinence during the follow-up period, 30 percent report they continue use and admit problems related to use, and 30 percent report non-problematic use. However, among those who report nonproblematic use, fully half meet diagnostic criteria for alcohol abuse or dependence." In other words, by collecting both self-reporting and factual information about consequences and diagnosis, a more complete picture emerges.

QUESTION ON PATIENT'S OVERALL PERSPECTIVE
OF ALCOHOL- OR DRUG-USE PROBLEM

In a similar vein, Hazelden has used the following item to gain patients' overall perspective of their alcohol- or drug-use problem. This item appeared in a longitudinal study of adolescents treated five years previously.

As compared to *(years, months)* ago, how would you now describe your problems with alcohol or other drugs?

_____ (1) a great deal better

_____ (2) somewhat better

_____ (3) no change

_____ (4) somewhat worse

_____ (5) much worse

Why? _____

Hazelden researchers found this item particularly informative as, surprisingly, most respondents described their problems as "a great deal better" or at least "somewhat better," even though they had returned to using alcohol or other drugs. To understand their perception of "better," the researchers added the follow-up question "Why" and, as a result, obtained a picture of what had improved for these youth and their families, which was clinically useful information. The researchers also learned that both parents and youth reported that the youths' problems were better, even though a proportion was using at levels that met *DSM-IV* criteria for abuse or dependence. This finding suggested new material for future study.

REASON FOR USE QUESTION

Program staff are often interested in the factors leading to relapse. Hazelden researchers have found it helpful to ask one relatively simple question about the patient's perception of the precipitating cause. Though this does not shed light on underlying causes (for instance, not attending AA meetings, not attending therapy, experiencing stressful life events), it may offer program staff ideas for overall treatment planning or aftercare services.

(If used) Which one of these was most directly related to your first use of alcohol or other drugs (not including nicotine)? (One response only)

_____ (1) craving

_____ (2) impulsive action, spur-of-the-moment decision

_____ (3) social/peer pressure

_____ (4) anxious, nervous mood

_____ (5) depressed, distressed mood

_____ (6) tense or difficult situation

_____ (7) happy or exciting situation

_____ (8) weighed the consequences and decided the risks were minimal

_____ (9) other (describe): _____

RISK FOR RELAPSE QUESTION

Finally, some stakeholders may be interested in the rate of risk for relapse among former patients. A scale called AWARE (Assessment of WArning signs for RElapse) can be used to assess relapse risk.[6] Based on Terence Gorski's relapse-prevention model,[7] AWARE includes twenty-eight items that reflect a person's overall emotional state, confidence in staying sober, and problematic behaviors. Examples of items include "I get irritated or annoyed with my friends," "I have good eating habits," "I think about drinking," and "I am doing things to stay sober." They are scored on a Likert Scale from 1 to 7, ranging from "never" to "always." A Likert Scale, named after Renis Likert, is simply a scale that shows a progression of values, such as from "low" to "high," from "not at all" to "very much," or from "poor" to "excellent," and is usually given to measure attitudes or beliefs. AWARE has a high level of internal consistency, meaning that the items "hang together" quite well. This suggests they are all part of the same construct. This scale also has some established predictive validity, meaning it correlates with or predicts future drinking behavior. AWARE's authors point out that it may also provide information about overall level of "sobriety" or quality of recovery beyond basic abstinence. The full AWARE scale can be found in appendix 4.

Treatment and Recovery History

Analyzing patients' outcomes in light of their previous experience with treatment and recovery can be helpful. Generally, outcomes are the most favorable after the first treatment, with slightly decreasing recovery rates with subsequent treatments.[8] However, the relationship between treatment outcome and prior history is likely to be complex and may depend on whether a person benefited for any significant period from a previous treatment episode. While no standardized instruments have been designed specifically to measure this domain, the following areas are important to gather information about at time of baseline: number of previous inpatient or residential treatments; number of previous outpatient treatments; length of each treatment; number of treatments completed; and length of abstinence after each treatment. In terms of overall recovery history, it may be helpful to gather information about length of longest sobriety after disease onset and methods the patient used to sustain that abstinence.

At time of follow-up, it is also important to capture the number and types of treatment services used after treatment. Some services—such as transfer to a halfway house from primary treatment or attendance at an outpatient program or continuing care group—are a continuation of treatment and a sign that a patient is continuing to make progress. Still, a totally new inpatient or outpatient episode may indicate that the initial treatment stay was unsuccessful and the patient relapsed. Therefore, when information about further alcohol and drug treatment is collected at follow-up, be careful to differentiate between continued treatment and new treatment.

Mental Health

As more patients come to treatment with co-occurring disorders, there is greater recognition that mental health problems play a role in relapse. One option for measuring overall mental health functioning is the Structured Clinical Interview for DSM-IV Personality Disorders (SCID-II).[9] SCID is lengthy and can be quite time-consuming to administer. It also takes special training to use. However, it offers the assurance that good information about diagnosis is being collected.

Another tool for measuring overall mental health functioning is the Behavior and Symptom Identification Scale (BASIS-32).[10] BASIS-32, as its name reflects, is a thirty-two-item, self-administered questionnaire that uses a Likert Scale from 0 to 4 for evaluating functioning in day-to-day life and at home, work, and school. In addition, it includes items covering symptoms of mood and thought disorders. BASIS-32 is not in the public domain, but Susan Eisen, the developer, typically allows clinical providers to use the instrument at no cost.

Measurement tools are also available for disorders in which there is particular interest. For example, depression is the most common mental health problem among people treated for alcohol or drug abuse. A standardized, relatively easy instrument to use is the Center for Epidemiological Studies-Depression (CES-D) scale.[11] It is easy to administer, with only twenty items. While originally developed for epidemiological work rather than for clinical diagnosis, it yields useful information about signs and symptoms of depression and is gaining widespread acceptance. A copy of the CES-D is provided in appendix 5.

The Beck Depression Inventory, or BDI,[12] is perhaps the most widely used screening tool for depression, which makes it a particularly useful questionnaire for comparison. It is also short, consisting of twenty-one self-reporting items. However, it takes somewhat longer to administer by telephone as the response options are varied. The BDI is copyrighted, and there is a charge for its use.

SCID also contains sections relevant to specific disorders. For example, if there is particular concern about attention deficit hyperactivity disorder (ADHD) among a sample being followed subsequent to adolescent treatment, the section of SCID aimed at ADHD could be used.

Quality of Life and Relationships

Quality of life indicators are key for evaluating changes that are assumed to accompany abstinence. However, quality of life is notoriously difficult to measure, as what constitutes quality of life depends entirely on a person's perception of life and self-report. The good news is that results are consistent, that is, most patients report the same thing (improved quality of life after treatment, regardless of their alcohol- or drug-use status). While quality of life may not be a hard-and-fast barometer of success, items in this domain probably tap into how well a person is functioning socially and emotionally in his or her day-to-day life.

There are several options to choose from in measuring quality of life and related variables. The Life Situation Survey (LSS) is a twenty-item instrument, with each item scored on a Likert Scale from 1 to 7.[13] Total scores can range from 20 to 140, with scores below 90 in the "poor" range. For purposes of outcome measurement, the scores are best used in comparing quality of life before and after treatment, or in detecting incremental change over the course of recovery. The categories include sleep, self-esteem, health, earnings, nutrition, autonomy, stress, social nurturance, work/life role, environment, leisure, energy level, egalitarianism, mood/affect, love/affection, mobility, public support, security, outcome, and social support. In one study, relapse was associated with diminution in mood/affect, work/life role, and public support.[14] Conversely, improvements in self-esteem, sleep, and nutrition were more likely among people who did not relapse to heavy drinking. This study is correlational, so it cannot be determined whether the improvements in quality of life caused or

TABLE 3.1

Quality of Life Question

On a scale of **1 to 7**, please indicate how satisfied you have been with each area of your life since treatment.

1 = Very Dissatisfied,   **7** = Very Satisfied,   **NA** = Not Applicable

1. Recreation, social activities

NA 1 2 3 4 5 6 7

2. Relationship with friends

NA 1 2 3 4 5 6 7

3. Relationship with children

NA 1 2 3 4 5 6 7

4. Relationship with parents

NA 1 2 3 4 5 6 7

5. Relationship with spouse or partner

NA 1 2 3 4 5 6 7

6. Overall quality of life

(1) Much improved

(2) Somewhat improved

(3) About the same

(4) Somewhat worse

(5) Much worse

resulted from changes in drinking. However, having these quality of life indicators in a follow-up study helps complete the picture of what happens to people in sobriety or in continued drinking.

Table 3.1 on page 38 shows the quality of life question Hazelden uses. Items 1–5 cover specific categories and item 6 is a general quality of life question.

Employment

The ability to maintain consistent employment and adequate job performance is another important indicator of successful treatment. This can sometimes be hard to capture as some patients are self-employed or are only scheduled to work periodically.

Hazelden uses the following question, based in part on the ASI, to help assess employment status:

What is your current (past thirty days) employment status? (One response only)

(1) full-time (at least thirty-five hours per week)

(2) part-time (regular hours)

(3) part-time (irregular day work)

(4) part-time student, part-time employed

(5) student

(6) service (military)

(7) homemaker

(8) retired/disability

(9) unemployed

(10) in controlled environment (jail, hospital, treatment center)

The following questions help to get a picture of a person's functioning on the job before and after treatment. At the start of treatment, the patient gives information in the first column about the year before treatment. Then, the identical question is asked at follow-up about the year after treatment. Researchers at Hazelden have asked patients at follow-up to estimate both time periods. Although patients seem to have good memory for both periods, at best, these are "ballpark" figures; validity and reliability studies would strengthen these questions.

	Number of times in the year *before* treatment	Number of times *since* treatment
Unplanned absences from work? (for example, called in sick, car broke down, etc.)		
Disciplined on the job?		
Job been in jeopardy? (for example, been warned you may lose your job)		
Suspended or fired from a job?		

Legal Situation

Some of the best indicators of legal problems, or lack thereof, come from the Addiction Severity Index. While you may choose not to administer the entire ASI, using items from the legal section may be especially important if you are measuring a population with a large number of legal problems and/or where improvements in legal status are expected after treatment. While the legal section does not have stand-alone validity, and it is not ideal to pull individual items from a standardized questionnaire, you must make judicious compromises from time to time. In published studies, you sometimes see researchers using only selected sections of the ASI and SCID since they are so long. At a minimum, items about driving while intoxicated or driving under the influence (DWIs or DUIs), number of other arrests, and number of days in jail are good gauges of a person's recovery. A caveat regarding number of days in jail: In some populations, clients attend treatment with the understanding that jail time will follow. When aggregated, it may be difficult or impossible to tell if the relatively high number of jail days after treatment is due to new offenses or if the jail time is simply the consequence of an earlier offense.

Health

A key area of anticipated change during recovery is health functioning. An excellent measure of this is the Medical Outcomes Survey SF-12 (Short Form-12 Items) or SF-36 (Short Form-36 Items).[15] The Medical Outcomes health questionnaire was developed with a grant from the Kaiser Family Foundation to evaluate health status across a wide range of chronic illnesses. Six different categories of health and related functioning are assessed: physical functioning, role functioning, social functioning, pain, mental health, and health perception. The Medical Outcomes Survey (in numerous versions) has been normed and used on groups of people with depression, asthma, diabetes, hypertension, heart disease, migraine, and other illnesses.[16] More recently, a twenty-item version was used in a large-scale study of over 2,500 addicts and alcoholics in Boston. It was found to be reliable and to yield results that were surprisingly similar to the results for other disorders.[17] Compared with respondents for other diseases, alcoholics and addicts reported more difficulty in the areas of pain, mental health, and overall perception of health. One version of the Medical Outcomes Survey, the SF-12, is provided in appendix 6.

Spiritual Life

In Twelve Step programs such as Alcoholics Anonymous, changes in spirituality are expected to occur as a result of treatment and over the course of time in recovery. This makes such programs an excellent proximal indicator of treatment success. Researchers and clinicians alike have learned that, while AA attendance may be a good indicator of involvement, it is better to ask specific questions regarding AA Steps, sponsorship, and participation. The Steps Questionnaire is perhaps the most comprehensive questionnaire, with forty-two items focusing on the first three Steps of Alcoholics Anonymous.[18] It is copyrighted, though use is at no charge. Another detailed questionnaire is the fifty-three-item Brown-Peterson Recovery Progress Inventory, which focuses primarily on Step Four and beyond and related behaviors and thoughts.[19] Little research has been done on this instrument, but the content has high appeal for clinicians and may be useful in follow-up studies. Other useful instruments include the Attribution to God's Influence Scale (AGIS)[20] and the Surrender Scale.[21]

Two different brief surveys have been developed to measure overall involvement in Alcoholics Anonymous. The Alcoholics Anonymous Involvement (AAI) scale was developed by Scott Tonigan and his colleagues as part of the instrument development for Project MATCH.[22] The AAI includes items about number of AA meetings attended, AA birthdays, AA sponsorship, number of Steps worked, and spiritual awakening. A similar scale was developed by Keith Humphreys and his colleagues, called the Alcoholics Anonymous Affiliation Scale (AAAS).[23] This is a shorter scale, with nine yes-or-no items, covering number of AA meetings attended, calling an AA member for help, service work, reading AA literature, and sponsorship. It is very easy to score. The AAI and AAAS are provided in appendixes 7 and 8. John

Allen, a researcher with the National Institute on Alcohol Abuse and Alcoholism during the Project MATCH study, has written a good overview of AA-related process measures, reviewing several of the above instruments.[24]

In addition to instruments that focus on Twelve Step programs to measure spiritual growth, much work has been done on in-depth measurement of spirituality and changes in beliefs. More information on methods and instruments is available in several sources, including a Web site maintained by the Center on Alcoholism, Substance Abuse, and Addictions (CASAA) at the University of New Mexico (casaa.unm.edu/bib/fetzer.html) and the book *Measures of Religiosity*, edited by Peter Hill and Ralph Hood.[25]

Improved Social/Community Functioning; Prosocial Behavior
An often-overlooked area of change after treatment is in the area of contribution to society. Improved alcoholics and addicts do not just reduce their problematic behavior, they increase their prosocial behavior. While some increases in prosocial behavior can be inferred from decreases in number of arrests and improvement in quality of life, the changes go beyond these domains into areas of community involvement. In a longitudinal study on adolescents moving into young adulthood after treatment, Hazelden used the following questions:

Are you a registered voter in your community?

1 = yes

2 = no

Did you vote in the last primary election, which is typically in September?

1 = yes

2 = no

Did you vote in the local and national elections in November?

1 = yes

2 = no

During the past five years, have you

contributed time or money in support of a political candidate?

1 = yes

2 = no

served on a school government, policy, or social committee? (in high school or post–high school)

1 = yes

2 = no

participated in a church organization or activity (other than attending church services)?

1 = yes

2 = no

volunteered time to help a charity organization or to assist citizens in need?

1 = yes

2 = no

participated in a local neighborhood organization to improve the neighborhood's quality of life or to address a neighborhood problem?

1 = yes

2 = no

These types of items may be useful in measuring and conveying a picture of recovery beyond problem abatement.

Creating Your Own Questions

In some cases, the information you need is unique and not readily available in an already-established questionnaire. While it is best to use standardized instruments when possible, most programs find they need to add special items. Keep in mind several considerations when constructing your own questions.

- Make sure that each item addresses only one concept. For example, the following item is poorly constructed: "I have a job that I like and work at forty hours a week." If a respondent answers "false," it is impossible to determine if the person (a) does not have a job; (b) does not like his or her job; or (c) does not work at least forty hours a week. Either ask three different, short questions, addressing each aspect, or decide in which aspect you are most interested and simply address that.

- Avoid leading questions. The way you phrase a question should not influence the direction of the response. For example, the question "How well did we help you?" pulls for positive responses. A more neutral question such as "To what extent did we or did we not help you?" would be more likely to produced unbiased responses.

- Make sure the language in the questions is easily understood. Avoid jargon. For example, you may think a question such as "Did you connect with your community provider after treatment?" is perfectly clear. A typical respondent might be confused about the meaning of "community provider" and need the term defined more specifically, such as "a local therapist or counseling clinic." This is where pilot testing, or trying out the items on a few people who are not involved in the project, can be helpful.

- Keep most items closed ended rather than open ended, especially for most large sample surveys. A closed-ended item gives a person a choice of responses such as "yes" or "no" or asks the person to choose from a series of responses such as "very good, good, fair, poor." An open-ended question—such as "How would you describe your relationship with your family since treatment?"—asks for the respondent's own words. Closed-ended questions can be used to calculate quantitative data. They produce information that is easier to examine and report using statistical methods. They also take less time to ask and analyze. However, it's useful to include some open-ended questions in your survey. Open-ended questions give qualitative or narrative data and can be used to supplement the quantitative data. Still, keep the open-ended items to a minimum. Asking many open-ended questions creates difficulty for the interviewers to capture information accurately and control the interview so that it does not stray into unproductive areas or take an overly long amount of time.

Response Options

Closed-ended questions require developing response options. In general, it is better to construct items or scales that have a wide range of responses. For example, let's suppose you want to obtain information about a person's job satisfaction. You could ask, "Do you like your job?" and get a yes-or-no answer. However, it would be better to ask, "Which of the following describes your level of satisfaction with your job?" and offer response options from 1 to 7, with 1 being "very satisfied" and 7 being "not satisfied at all." Giving a wide range of options is better for two reasons. First, offering more categories from which to choose may result in more accuracy. Second, statistically, you will have more variety in responses, which may help in analysis. If there is a severe restriction in range, you may find very few significant differences between groups, not because there was no difference, but because people had very little room to move. For example, in the above item, you may find subtle differences between people who have abstained and people who have relapsed. Both may be fairly satisfied with their jobs, but those who have abstained may score, on the average, 1.2 while those who have relapsed may score 2.4. A statistical test may even find a statistically significant difference between these two scores. However, if you had simply asked the yes-or-no question, you may find that the majority of both groups answer yes and thus miss the differences between the groups.

A common debate is whether there should be an even number of responses, such as 1 to 4, with 1 being "excellent" and 4 being "poor," or an odd number of responses, such as 1 to 5, with 1 being "excellent," 3 being "neutral" (or unwilling to commit or undecided), and 5 being "poor." The crux of the argument is whether people should have the "middle" or undecided option and, if so, how that response should be interpreted. Different researchers have their own preferences, and there is no universally accepted solution to the debate. The best solution is to think ahead and imagine the results you may obtain with your response categories. Are you comfortable interpreting them? Do they make sense to you and your audience? Answers to these questions are probably the best guides to determining whether your response categories should be even or odd numbers. Appendix 9 contains a collection of common response categories.

Finally, make sure the question and the response categories match. For example, if the question addresses frequency of a behavior, such as drinking or using, the response items should be phrased specifically in terms of "how often" and not "how much." If the question asks specifically about satisfaction, the response categories must be phrased in terms of satisfaction rather than helpfulness. For example, if a patient were asked to rate the following items on a scale of *excellent, good, fair, poor,* only the first two items make sense.

> My relationship with my family:
>   excellent, good, fair, poor

> My ability to do my job:
>   excellent, good, fair, poor

> Problems with stress:
>   excellent, good, fair, poor

The response choices for the third item don't provide any information. If the response is "excellent," you do not know if the person has had no stress problems or if he or she has had many stress problems but believes they are being handled in an excellent way. Instead, it would be better to phrase the item "My ability to handle stress." This way the response categories would be consistent with the question. While it seems obvious that the question and the response categories should flow naturally from one to the other, disjointed question-response categories can creep into a questionnaire during revisions.

Testing Your Questionnaire

Before using your questionnaire, conduct a pilot test to see if it's going to work the way you want it to work. In a pilot test, you try the items out on a small sample of patients that are similar to the actual sample you will be studying. A pilot test helps you learn how well respondents understand the items and whether the items produce the information you expect.

How to Conduct a Pilot Test

Gather a group of patients similar to those who will ultimately be using the questionnaire. For example, if you will be following up patients one year after treatment, test the items with recovering people who are about one year out of treatment. If the questionnaire is going to be administered verbally, conduct the pilot test verbally, not by paper and pencil or some other method.

When you have gathered the pilot-test participants, explain that you would like them to answer the questions quietly without discussion, and that you'd like them to stay and talk about the questionnaire after everybody has finished it. When all the respondents have completed the questionnaire, engage them in a discussion about each item and about the questionnaire as a whole. For each question ask, "In your own words, what was I asking here?" Listen to their responses. Ask if the format made sense, if they had any difficulty with the response categories or instructions, or if they thought the scale was too long.

The information from a pilot test can be surprisingly simple, yet helpful. For example, you may learn that several people missed what you thought were clear instructions to skip items or turn pages. Even if you are using a standardized instrument (in which case you will not be modifying the items), pilot testing can still help to uncover problems in format, timing, or instructions.

In summary, designing a good questionnaire involves understanding the key domains you need to cover, making a serious effort to simplify the scope of the project and shorten the questionnaire while still gathering adequate information, using appropriate, already-established instruments, using new questions in a way that does not compromise the integrity of your results, and pilot testing the end result. Even after following this thorough process, remain open to making changes or revisions in the early stages of the project. The key to ending up with good data and a great report is asking the right questions from the beginning.

4

Implementing the Outcome Study

So far we have looked at the overall planning process for an outcome study, asking these questions: Who wants to know the information produced by the study, what do they want to know, and when do they want to know it? We have talked about considering exactly what you want to measure—the outcome indicators or variables—and how to define them. Finally, we have discussed how to develop a questionnaire suited to your particular outcome study, using standardized instruments or a mixture of standardized instruments and specially designed questions. In this chapter, we will look, first, at beginning the study; second, at collecting information during treatment; third, at setting up a system to collect information after treatment; and, finally, at administering the questionnaire.

Beginning the Study

Before contacting that first potential patient for your outcome study, you still need to consider a couple of things. These include, first, how you make the initial patient contact and, second, how you will gather baseline data.

Initial Patient Contact

The first step in conducting the study is to invite the clients or patients to participate. This involves securing their consent to be in the study and getting information on how to contact them in the future. The best time to obtain this is at the beginning of treatment.

Consent to Participate

The primary purpose of securing patients' consent is to ensure their safety and guarantee confidentiality. Request that each person sign a consent form giving his or her permission to be a participant. For youth under the age of eighteen, a parent generally needs to sign the permission form. The consent form should include the following points of information:

- A statement that you are conducting a research study
- Purpose of the study and how long the respondent is expected to participate
- Procedures that will be used
- Any risks or discomfort
- Any benefits
- How records will be kept confidential
- Name and number of a person to contact about the project
- A statement that participation is voluntary and refusal to participate or a desire to discontinue participation at any time will not affect the client's treatment experience or relationship with his or her provider in any way

If your outcome study is being done by an organization that receives funds from the Department of Health and Human Services (DHHS), an arm of the federal government, it must be reviewed and monitored by a National Institutes of Health Institutional Review Board (IRB). In that case, you must include the above components in your consent form. Most university-based programs fall under this provision, as do many prison systems. In fact, if a university-based researcher is doing research or conducting outcomes at your organization, he or she most likely needs to follow IRB guidelines. More information about IRB and their requirements can be found at ohsr.od.nih.gov. If you have any questions about whether IRB regulations pertain to you, check with your

administration or access the Web site to learn more. You may
also be subject to confidentiality requirements put forth in the
Health Insurance Portability and Accountability Act (HIPAA).
More information on this can be found at aspe.hhs.gov.

Locator Form

It is helpful to obtain accurate contact information at the same
time that you ask patients for their consent to participate. You
can fill this information out on a "locator form." Get the name,
address, and phone number where participants can be
reached after treatment. Ideally, you will also be able to get
names and phone numbers of significant others who are likely
to know where participants are if they cannot be reached. The
patient should sign the locator form, giving you permission to
contact the people listed. The locator form should also ask the
patient's permission to disclose to contact people that you are
calling from the treatment program and to ask questions
about the patient's recovery process if necessary.

Gathering Baseline Data

Baseline data is the information gathered on the patient
to which post-treatment information is compared in order
to determine if treatment caused improvement. It is critical to
gather the same information at the time patients enter treatment and at the time they begin follow-up in order to answer
the question "Compared to what?" While you may "know" that
all your patients were drinking or using heavily at the outset
of treatment, and that they had major life problems in multiple
areas, it is far better to measure and report this information
factually than to leave it as an assumption. When gathering
information at intake, capture data about the period before
treatment that matches your outcome period. For example, if
you are planning to measure outcomes at one year after treatment you need to gather baseline information about the one
year before entry into treatment.

There are two ways you can gather this data. The first is to cull information from patients' medical records that is already being collected for clinical purposes. This can be a time-consuming process and may or may not yield the information you need. The second and preferable way is to administer the outcome study questionnaire you have developed. The questionnaire obtains information directly from patients, making the data more readily available for analysis and more comparable in format to information gathered later. This increases accuracy.

As mentioned in chapter 2, you will also need to gather additional one-time-only information, including basic demographic information (specifically, age, gender, race/ethnicity, and educational level); age of first use of alcohol or drugs; and age of first problem.

Collecting Information during Treatment

Information on progress in early recovery is probably the most critical but least understood measured aspect of treatment outcome. Collecting information during treatment is difficult. Patients and staff are immersed in the treatment process and may be busy completing forms and doing charting for other purposes. Filling out more forms for outcome research can seem onerous. Still, information collected during treatment with research in mind can serve two valuable purposes. First, it can be a record of progress, and second, it can help predict outcomes.

Table 4.1 on page 55 provides an example of patient information recorded during treatment. The "Patient's In-treatment Rating Scale" is used by TRIAD,[1] an alcohol and drug treatment program in the corrections system in Minnesota. This scale can have both clinical and research utility.

TABLE 4.1

Patient's In-treatment Rating Scale

Overall rating of client's participation in this treatment program:

	Exceeds Expectations	Meets Expectations	Does Not Meet Expectations
1. Attitude	☐ (2) Consistently positive attitude toward treatment, encouraged same in others	☐ (1) Positive attitude with occasional struggles	☐ (0) Undermining or negative view
2. Compliance	☐ (2) Consistently followed rules, held others accountable	☐ (1) Followed rules, held others accountable occasionally	☐ (0) Resistant, apathetic, excessive rule infractions
3. Self-discipline	☐ (2) Consistently showed self-control, self-challenging behavior	☐ (1) Exercised self-control with occasional struggles	☐ (0) Lacked self-restraint; was reactive
4. Responsibility	☐ (2) Consistent follow-through, self-directed, and accountable	☐ (1) Responsible, occasionally struggled with accountability	☐ (0) Lacked follow-through, blaming
5. Participation	☐ (2) Active in group/community, assisted/encouraged same in others	☐ (1) Moderate activity in group and community	☐ (0) Minimal activity, did bare minimum, superficial
6. Self-disclosure	☐ (2) Consistently took risks, open and honest, encouraged same in others	☐ (1) Moderate self-disclosure, shared with prompting or some encouragement	☐ (0) Closed, rigid, safe in self-disclosure
7. Assignments	☐ (2) Consistently done on time with depth, sought extra assignments	☐ (1) Completed on time with acceptable content	☐ (0) Often late, lacked depth or content
8. Overall	☐ (2)	☐ (1)	☐ (0)

While the scale needs to undergo further psychometric work to determine reliability and validity, it has proven clinically helpful in the TRIAD program. At the same time, this type of objective information could also add to researchers' general understanding of outcomes. For instance, it might answer the question "Are patients who make good progress in treatment, as rated by their counselors, more likely to have better outcomes?"

At a minimum, information collected during treatment should include the amount of services received in days or hours and discharge status, that is, whether a patient completed treatment satisfactorily. You can also gather information on staff ratings of progress during treatment, the nature and amount of services received during treatment, or patient satisfaction with treatment. It is also important to know whether patients adhered to their continuing care plan immediately after treatment, which generally includes self-help meetings and counseling.

Collecting Information after Treatment

Collecting the follow-up information is the heart of the study. You need to set up and test a system for doing this. First, we will look at choosing a method to administer the questionnaire; next, at training interviewers; and, finally, at testing the system.

Methods for Administering the Questionnaire

To collect follow-up information, various methods can be used, such as telephone interviews, mail, in-person interviews, and automated Web-based surveys.

Telephone Interviews

Administering the questionnaire by telephone is the most common method of collecting follow-up information. A "live" interviewer generally does this. The interviewer may be hired specifically to conduct the follow-up survey. Another option is to have a clinical staff person who is conducting clinical case management act as the interviewer for the questionnaire as well. This method is referred to as "utilization-focused evaluation."[2] Finally, systems have been developed using an automated interviewer, in which case clients are coached through a series of responses using their telephone keypad.

Hazelden researchers have found that separating outcome follow-up from case management follow-up works best, unless the follow-up is for a small sample or with a group of clinicians who have the time and interest to be involved in a research project. Utilization-focused evaluation has some advantages. It keeps the patients engaged with clinical staff, helps the clinical staff stay informed of challenges patients face as they transition out of the treatment environment, structures the interview, and saves resources by doubling the counselors' time as data collectors. However, there are distinct disadvantages as well. The resulting information may be unevenly obtained across the population and may reflect a great deal of subjectivity. Not all counselors are able or willing to diligently follow patients at all required points in time, especially if they have heavy caseloads of current patients with immediate needs. In addition, even when they are able to reach patients for case management, the conversation may not be directed specifically at the items needed for evaluation.

Mail

Mailed surveys often yield a low return and need to be paired with telephone follow-up of those who do not return their surveys in a prescribed amount of time. While at one time mailed surveys were common, they are now rarely used. However, one useful function for mail is to alert participants. A letter can be sent ahead of the telephone interview, reminding them that someone will be calling within the next two weeks to conduct the outcome interview. If clients cannot be located by phone, sometimes mail forwarded to a new address will reach them. In this way, they can be notified of their follow-up time and be asked to call the interviewer.

In-person Interviews

In-person interviews are feasible if clients live fairly close to the treatment center where the outcome study is done. Interviewers may go to clients' homes or clients may return to the clinic. In studies of homeless or very poor populations, interviewers may need to conduct an interview on the street, in a park, or in other places where their clientele live. They may also need to offer monetary or other incentives to boost response rates. For example, a research arm of a clinic might provide day care or Laundromat services onsite in order to retain people for follow-up. More typically, a meal coupon could be provided for people who return for their follow-up interviews. To avoid biasing the results, it is important that respondents understand that the incentive is simply for being interviewed, and is not based on whether they report abstinence or good functioning.

Automated Web-Based Surveys

At this time, there are no published studies of follow-up information being collected via e-mails or Web-based surveys. Theoretically, however, a system could easily be designed where automatic e-mails are sent out to clients at set times, reminding them of their follow-up survey date and providing a link to a Web-based survey that they could complete with full security. In turn, the surveys could be automatically aggregated into a continuously updated database and periodic reports.

Training Interviewers

Standardization is critical to successful outcome system implementation. In chapter 3, we discussed the careful effort that goes into constructing a standardized questionnaire. It is equally important that the questions are asked in standardized ways as well. In order to ensure standardization, staff should be provided scripts for various situations in which they may find themselves. The scripts should always be short and to the point.

Interviewer Scripts

Here are examples of common situations and scripts that can help interviewers respond to various situations in consistent, helpful ways.

- Locating patients without divulging confidentiality.

  "Hello. May I please speak to _____ ?"

  If asked why or where you are calling from, respond, *"I am doing a survey"* or *"I am doing an important health care survey and need to speak specifically with _____ ."* If the patient is unavailable, ask, *"Is this the typical phone number where she or he can be reached, or is there a better one?"* or *"Could you tell me a good time to call when I might be able to get hold of _____ directly?"*

- Introducing the study to the patient on the telephone. Use this script once it is established that you are, in fact, speaking to the former patient.

  "Hello, Max. I'm calling from Program _____ and would like to take about ten minutes of your time to ask a few questions about how things are going for you. As part of our ongoing evaluation, we call all patients six months after treatment. Is this a good time?" If the patient says, *"Yes,"* say, *"Great. I'll go through each question and ask*

that you be as honest with your responses as you can." Or, *"You might recall while you were in treatment, we talked about our evaluation process, where we call everyone six months after treatment to see how things are going. It's been six months since you left treatment at Program _____ and now I'd like to go through the questionnaire with you. Your responses are very important to us and I hope you'll be as honest as you can be."*

- Introducing each new section in the survey.

  For example, a section of the questionnaire labeled "Cost-Indicator Items" may contain items about medical, legal, and employment consequences. It would be better to remove that label and, instead, add in the script for the interviewers, *"Now I would like to ask a few questions about your work situation."*

Handling Potentially Difficult Situations

In every outcome study, interviewers will face unexpected, difficult situations. Interviewers will need to know what to do, for example, in response to a patient who has relapsed. Will they offer services? If so, whom should the patient call? Can they refer the patient, with the patient's permission, immediately to a clinical staff? What about a person who is apparently intoxicated at the time of the phone call? What if a patient makes violent threats? What about a patient (or family member) who has an angry complaint about the provider?

Think through these problematic situations, discuss them with all relevant parties, agree on a course of action, and train interviewers on the best ways to respond. In any case, the evaluation interviewer should never cross the boundary into counseling or providing advice to the respondent. This stricture can be especially difficult for interviewers who are in a program of recovery themselves, who are alumni of the program, or who feel a special pull toward helping others. The clearer the options and instructions, the better the interviewer will be able to provide good resources for the troubled patient while maintaining his or her own role and boundaries.

Testing Your System

Just as you pilot-tested your questionnaire, you should also pilot-test the system that carries out the study and administers the questionnaire. Plan for the first three to six participants to be test cases. For these patients, assume you will not get useable data for your outcome study; instead, you will be learning how well the process works. For example, if you plan to collect baseline data by recruiting and interviewing patients shortly after intake, do so and observe how well the procedures go. Are you finding out about new admits and potential participants in a timely way? Who is your contact person to let you know when a new patient has arrived? Is there a backup person? Are your materials filed for easy access and confidentiality?

Similarly, observe how well the process works when contact is made with the first three to six patients at outcome. Where is the patient log kept that tells the interviewers who needs to be contacted? If several interviewers are tracking the same group of patients, is there an easy way for them to share information with each other? The best procedures for gathering baseline and outcome data will be unique to each setting. As you establish them for your clinic, compile a procedures manual so that methods stay consistent and new staff can be consistently trained.

Administering the Questionnaire

Once you have decided on the method to collect information, trained your interviewers, tested your system, invited patients to participate, and obtained their consent, you can begin the actual follow-up. Administering the questionnaire requires deciding who to call in what order and exactly when, keeping track of the responses, and monitoring the process closely. In the following section, we will discuss these issues as well as how to anticipate and address the myriad of unexpected challenges that are bound to occur as you implement the study.

Scheduling Contacts

You need to have an accurate, methodical system in place to determine who gets a phone call (or other kinds of contact) and at what time intervals. Follow-up should be targeted at all patients consecutively discharged from the treatment program unless there is a specific reason to do otherwise. This is sometimes referred to as an "intent-to-treat" sample, meaning that no one is excluded from the outcome study even if they left treatment early or received an unfavorable discharge. You can construct either a simple database or a computer program to track which patients are eligible for contact, which have been called, and which are ready for their next call. For each patient, the interviewer should record the time and date of a phone attempt, whether anyone was reached and who, and what information was obtained about good contact times in the next day or two. Sometimes a family member will comment spontaneously on the patient's recovery, stating that the patient is abstinent and doing well or, conversely, that the patient has relapsed and is not doing well. While every attempt should be made to reach the patient, take notes on the family member's comments in case they become the only information obtainable.

Establishing Time Frames for Contacts

You also need to set a window of time during which a phone call or other contact with a participant can be made. For example, if a person is scheduled to receive a six-month phone call on the tenth of the month, it is unlikely that an interviewer will be able to reach the person on that exact day of the sixth month. On the other hand, if a person unexpectedly but belatedly returns the interviewer's phone call at the nine-month mark, is that better counted as a six-month outcome or a twelve-month outcome? At Hazelden, the following periods are used for beginning and ending interview attempts with patients:

- one-month data collection point: 25 to 44 days post-discharge
- six-month data collection point: 165 to 210 days post-discharge
- twelve-month data collection point: 350 to 395 days post-discharge

Since reaching all patients within the established time frame can be difficult, interviewers should begin phone call attempts at the earliest date allowed in the window of opportunity.

Tracking Responses

Keeping track of the reasons for noncontact is critically important. All patients must be accounted for when you have finished collecting data in order to calculate the response rate. The response rate is simply the proportion of actual clients contacted from the pool of eligible clients. If 100 patients were admitted to treatment program X, and 50 were successfully contacted, the response rate is 50 percent. Generally, response rates of at least 70 percent are needed for the study. Response rates of 80 percent, of course, are even better, and often attainable. (Project MATCH, the large multi-site national study funded by the NIAAA in 1989, obtained response rates in the mid-to-high nineties.) Tracking reasons for noncontact is also helpful in understanding how the outcome system might be improved to reach more patients. Hazelden uses the following categories in keeping track of reasons for nonresponse:

A. Could not locate

B. Located, patient refused to participate

C. Located, but patient could not be contacted
   for interview

   C1. No information available about status

   C2. Patient's contact states patient is abstinent

   C3. Patient's contact states patient has relapsed

D. Patient is deceased

   D1. Cause of death unknown

   D2. Cause of death alcohol- or drug-related

   D3. Cause of death not alcohol- or drug-related

E. Patient is in a post-primary treatment program
   (continued stay); abstinence is terms for remaining
   in program so abstinence is assumed

F. Patient is in a primary treatment program
   (retreatment), so relapse is assumed

G. Patient interviewed

You will need to adapt the categories for your own outcome system, of course.

Using the above categories, the most conservative response rate would be:

$$\text{Response rate} = G/\text{Total sample}$$

This response rate formula should be used in reporting treatment outcome results. In other words, unless a patient was interviewed personally, he or she was counted as missing. For example, if your total sample size was 100 and you interviewed 50 patients (G), your response rate is 50/100, or 50 percent.

In a less stringent computation of response rate, C2, C3, D2, D3, E, F, and G could be counted as patient information, resulting in a higher response rate and producing the formula:

Response rate = (C2+C3+D2+D3+E+F+G)/Total sample

In this formula, even though every attempt is made to reach a patient, data from other sources is accepted.

Unfortunately, the interviewer may learn of a patient's death from a family member during a routine follow-up phone call. The interviewer should simply respond by extending sympathy and later remove the patient from the patient log to avoid future attempts at contact. The family member may volunteer cause of death (for instance, by suicide or overdose), or the interviewer may be able to inquire in a tactful way about the cause of death. This is very helpful information in understanding the overall picture of outcomes, especially if the death is alcohol- or drug-related.

Monitoring the Interviews

Once the interviews begin, plan to monitor the whole process carefully. Find out answers to questions such as "How long does a typical interview take?" "Are the interviewers able to gather the information accurately and well?" "What kinds of questions do they have?" and "Are the questionnaires readily available?" Review the completed forms daily to ensure that each interviewer understands how to complete the items for accurate data entry. (How to check the data collection is discussed in more detail in chapter 5.) Meet with staff briefly during each shift to review errors and decide on ways to avoid them in the future. For example, callers may be using pencil instead of ink, which will make the responses difficult to read at time of data entry, or they may be reporting the responses in narrative form ("one or two times"), instead of checking off one of the boxes.

Meet with the interviewers as a group at least once a week to answer questions and address common concerns. Keep track of decisions made so you can pass them on to interviewers who could not attend the meeting and as a reminder to yourself when you sit down to interpret the data and write up the results. During group meetings, the following types of questions are likely to be posed:

- "What if a respondent can't choose between two responses?" For example, if the response categories call for a person to name their primary drug of choice, and they say they have two drugs of choice, which should be used? Or, if the response categories include options of employment and education, and the person responds by saying they work half-time and go to school half-time, which response should be marked?

- "What is really meant by (a particular term)?" For example, if the respondent is currently on a leave of absence, does that still count as "employed"? In the section about family, for a young adult who's living with a new spouse and baby, does "family" refer to her family of origin or to her current living situation?

While you no doubt made every attempt to construct questions and responses that avoid these dilemmas, they will inevitably occur. The best solution is to agree on a systematic way to code the data or prompt the respondent, document it, and monitor future questionnaires to make sure consistency is maintained. (At Hazelden, the supervisor of the interviewers sends out a short e-mail informing everyone of the clarification, documents it in an ongoing log, and monitors incoming questionnaires.) If it is early in the study, it may be possible to modify the questionnaire. If modification is not possible, the need for changing an item or a response to improve clarity should be noted and incorporated into a future revision.

If it is relatively early in the study, or if there will be a natural break between this study and the next, such as outcomes for 2003 and a second wave of outcomes for 2004, you may be able to implement revisions in the questionnaire, clarifying the response categories and options. For example, in the items above, create a new response category saying "both employed and attending school," a new response category for being on a leave of absence, and specific directions asking respondents to think of their family as those people in their current living situation.

For these and other idiosyncratic questions, consult with similar or previous research studies with your population to see how they have been handled. If there are no previous records or examples to use as guidelines, decide the most logical approach, document it, and remain consistent. In some cases, you may be able to make a decision that is guided by the purpose of your study. For example, if you know you will be looking at the correlation between work and outcome, you may want to count the person who both works and goes to school as "employed." In other cases, there may be no guiding logic, and you will need to make an arbitrary decision. Again, the key is to be consistent.

Regular meetings with groups of interviewers can also help them deal with difficult situations or respondents. While you have prepared scripts for the basic and obvious interview situations, interviewers will have new questions about how to handle certain difficult or puzzling situations.

- What do you do if a person says they can't remember?
- What if you finally get them and they say they only have five minutes?
- What if you get in the middle of the questionnaire and they say they don't want to continue?
- What if I get the patient's mom (dad, spouse, etc.) and they want to tell me about how the person is doing, instead of letting me talk to the person?

Often, what is difficult for one interviewer may be easy for another. The more experienced interviewers will have stories to share about techniques they have tried. While you may not be able to create a script for difficult situations, you (or, even better, one of the interviewers) may be able to create a tip sheet.

The group meetings can also help with maintaining high response rates. Some interviewers will routinely have more success than others in reaching former clients. In group meetings, give the success stories a chance to be told. They may provide helpful advice about ways to locate respondents and successfully complete interviews. If someone completes a particularly high number of interviews in a certain week, let the person know you noticed. Formal or informal incentives can be built into compensation systems to reward groups or individuals for maintaining high response rates. Group incentives—rewarding everyone for the overall success of the project—work best. Incentives may be as simple as a free delivered lunch, such as pizza or sub sandwiches for the whole group, or small gift certificates to local restaurants or stores. Even posting the latest results can help remind everyone about the goal and progress toward it. Tracking patients and obtaining follow-up information from people who may not always be treatment successes can be difficult work.

Providing incentives and rewards, even in small ways, helps keep the work environment a little lighter and demonstrates appreciation.

5

Presenting the Information

The information-gathering period is now over, but you still have a great deal of work to do. You have to sort through all those questionnaires and try to understand what they are telling you. You also have to figure out the best way to make the information available to the people who are interested in your study. You will need to put the information contained in the questionnaires into a clear and easy-to-understand report. In this chapter, we will look at how to analyze the data and how to write a report for internal audiences, using tables, charts, graphics, a narrative, and an appropriate format. We will also discuss a few observations about report writing for external audiences.

Analyzing the Data

Once you have gathered all the follow-up information from the study participants, you have to make sense of the data. There are three important steps in data analysis: (1) checking, cleaning, and coding the data; (2) entering the data; and (3) organizing the data into tables. We will look at each of these steps in turn.

Checking, Cleaning, and Coding the Data

Checking, cleaning, and coding the data is a critical component of the study and can make or break the integrity of the data. Many inexperienced researchers overlook this step, assuming their data are all set to go the minute the information is collected. If you're lucky, this will be true, but you absolutely cannot count on this being the case. It's far too easy for errors to creep into the process.

Checking the Data

Ideally, you checked the data during the entire data collection process. Each day, or at least each week, it is important to review the data collection forms for accuracy and consistency. This is especially important during the training period of a new interviewer and for everyone when a new project begins. Still, even when forms have been reviewed on an ongoing basis, errors or inconsistencies will sneak in. Before data entry, check that

- the entries are legible.
- there is only one response per item (unless otherwise called for).
- the entries make sense. For example, the date of first drink after treatment cannot be earlier than the discharge date from treatment.
- the pages are in place and in consecutive order.
- all the items are completed or, if not, a "missing data" code is used.

Cleaning the Data

Cleaning the data simply means correcting the raw data entries to eliminate obvious errors. For instance, a respondent who was asked to check off drugs she has used may have checked "other" and written "crack" next to the check mark. It would be appropriate to move this response to a category containing the drug cocaine, since crack is a form of cocaine and not an entirely different drug. Obviously, only bona fide errors can be corrected; item responses can never be changed.

Coding the Data

As part of the preparation for data entry, each questionnaire should be given a client code or case number. If the client already has a clinic history number or case number, that number can be used. However, if the data are leaving the premises for any part of the entry or analysis process, unique codes must be assigned to protect confidentiality. This can be as simple as giving consecutive three-digit numbers to everyone in the study alphabetically, for instance, #100 for Thea Ahren, #101 for Josh Beri, #102 for Jarrod Castle, etc. Keep a record of client codes in a separate codebook and put the codebook in a secure location.

Data Entry

Data entry, if done by hand, simply entails entering each item of the questionnaire into a database. The database can range from a simple Excel spreadsheet to a statistical analysis package such as Statistical Package for the Social Sciences (SPSS).[1] After data entry, the data need to be checked and cleaned again for integrity. Even the best data entry process may allow human errors into the system. There are several options for ensuring accuracy of data entry. The two most practical are double-checking and outlier review.

Double-Checking

Double-checking involves selecting a random sample of about 10 percent of your cases and comparing the raw data from the questionnaire with the data entered into the database. When there are few, if any, errors, you can be sure that your database is accurate or at least that no systematic errors in data entry have occurred. If you find numerous errors, continue checking and correcting until you are assured of an accurate database. If your sample is small and your questionnaire short, you could review all entries. If the interviewers enter data directly into an automated system, this method of checking data is not possible of course.

Outlier Review

Outliers are extreme scores, either high or low, or responses that are outside the expected range. Outliers may not be mistakes, but they do signal a need to double-check the raw data. For example, if you are evaluating outcomes at an adolescent program and you're finding ages significantly outside the range of twelve to eighteen, there is probably an error. Or if the data indicate that 50 percent of your patients are cocaine users and every other report or your clinical experience tells you that the rate should be closer to 20 percent, there may be an error. Once a potential error has been spotted, locate the case number or numbers and go back to the original questionnaire or data source to see if you can discover the problem and make the correction.

Some data entry software incorporates data-checking mechanisms. A common method used in software packages is range restriction. That is, if a number falls outside the defined range, the database will not accept it and signal the user. Another method used is double entry. Here, the data are entered twice, and mismatches in any field will be reported.

Writing the Report

When certain your data are accurate, prepare your report. There are many types of reports, ranging from internal reports to various types of external reports, such as monographs and journal articles. In preparing a report for a professional journal, hypotheses are formulated and statistical analyses are performed on the data. Each journal has its own guidelines for publication, and these should be consulted before embarking on writing.

For our purposes we are going to assume the audience is internal—board members, administration, and key staff—with less formal expectations. Still, there will be broad differences in how much information even this rather limited range of people will want and in what form. Some will want an overview of the main findings. Others appreciate more minute detail. Some will prefer descriptive narrative, while others will skip the narrative and look for tables and charts. To create a successful report, you will need to

- incorporate as much variety as possible, providing both narratives and visuals.
- summarize the main points in an executive summary at the beginning of the report and provide as much detail as possible in an appendix.
- develop a consistent, predictable format for your reports and repeat it across programs and over time. Modify the format as you receive feedback to make it user-friendly.

The elements that go into a report are covered below.

Tables and Graphs

Use tables and graphs to display the main pieces of information you want to convey. It is helpful to do the tables and graphs first because you can build your narrative around them. Here we will look at the primary types of illustrations to use in outcome reports.

Tables

Tables are the most elemental part of any report and a simple way to organize or list basic descriptive data and to convey relatively large quantities of numerical information. They typically contain frequencies or averages and are often used for displaying demographics, scale scores, and details of responses to selected variables. The following tables illustrate these functions.

DEMOGRAPHIC INFORMATION. Table 5.1 on page 76 shows how simple demographic information comparing two groups in an outcome study can be displayed.

TABLE 5.1

Characteristics of Patients Treated at Program X

CHARACTERISTICS	MALES (N=100)	FEMALES (N=55)
Age (mean)	32.8	44.6
Years of education (mean)	10.1	13.2
Number of dependents (mean)	1.3	2.8
Employed full-time (%)	36%	54%

The "N" in the column headers is a symbol for "number" and simply denotes sample size. "Mean," of course, is the average. If you are familiar with statistics, you can also put standard deviations in parentheses after the means. In comparing groups, you might do statistical analyses to see if the differences are statistically significant (that is, larger than could be attributed to chance). In Table 5.1, you would probably do a t-test to compare the means on the first three variables, and a chi-square test to compare the proportions on the last variable. (See the sidebar on t-tests and chi-square tests on page 77.)

SCALE SCORES. Tables are a good place to put details about scale scores. For example, if you obtained baseline and outcome data on the Addiction Severity Index (ASI), you might display the data as shown in table 5.2 on page 77.

In this table, program data (in the column labeled "Hazelden") are shown in comparison with other data (in this case labeled "DENS" and used from a database of alcohol/drug patients maintained by Deltametrics, an outcome monitoring company). Any published data or available data from other databases can be used for comparison. While it is a great benefit for the program to have comparative data, this may not always be possible, in which case the data for a program can be shown without comparison. Showing test scores in this fashion gives the reader a great deal of information in a small amount of space.

T-TESTS AND CHI-SQUARE TESTS

A t-test is a statistical test comparing averages of two groups. For example, a t-test might be used to compare the average age of men with the average age of women in a sample, or the average number of years of education between inpatients and outpatients. The results of a t-test tell you whether any difference between the two groups is likely to be due to chance.

A chi-square test is used on categorical data, and tells whether any apparent difference in proportions between two or more groups is due to chance or is real. For example, a chi-square test might be used to compare the proportion of drug users versus alcohol users in two groups, or the proportion of men versus women.

The results of these tests can be given in a separate column in the table, or asterisks can be used to indicate which comparisons are significant. If you plan to use statistical analyses in your report, consult a statistics textbook and/or knowledgeable colleagues to determine the best analyses to include and how to interpret them.

TABLE 5.2
Baseline Differences:
Hazelden Employed Males versus Inpatient/Residential DENS Males

VARIABLE	HAZELDEN (N=104) M (SD)	DENS (N=3968) M (SD)
Baseline Medical Composite Score	.09 (.23)	.18 (.30)
Baseline Employment Composite Score	.21 (.21)	.83 (.23)
Baseline Alcohol Composite Score	.59 (.30)	.33 (.31)
Baseline Drug Composite Score	.14 (.16)	.20 (.13)
Baseline Legal Composite Score	.07 (.15)	.16 (.21)
Baseline Family Composite Score	.30 (.24)	.18 (.20)
Baseline Psychiatric Composite Score	.31 (.24)	.18 (.23)

RESPONSES TO INDIVIDUAL ITEMS. Tables can be used to display responses to individual items. It is often too cumbersome to review each item response in narrative form.

TABLE 5.3

Item Responses to the Religious Background and Behaviors Questionnaire[2]

ITEM	NEVER	YES, IN THE PAST BUT NOT NOW	YES, AND I STILL DO
Believed in God (Higher Power)? (n=104)	6.7 (7)	12.5 (13)	80.8 (84)
Prayed? (n=105)	6.7 (7)	27.6 (29)	65.7 (69)
Meditated? (n=102)	31.4 (32)	28.4 (29)	40.2 (41)
Attended worship services regularly? (n=104)	20.2 (21)	60.6 (63)	19.2 (20)
Read scriptures or holy writings regularly? (n=104)	43.3 (45)	36.5 (38)	20.2 (21)
Had direct experiences with God (Higher Power)? (n=104)	38.5 (40)	25.0 (26)	36.5 (38)

In table 5.3, the number of people responding to each item is shown in the first column, immediately after the item; for example, "n=104" indicates that 104 people answered the question "Believed in God (Higher Power)?" The overall sample size was 105 people, but some respondents skipped some questions. In each subsequent column, the percent endorsing that response is shown first, followed by the number of people, in parentheses. For example, we can see that 6.7 percent or seven individuals report never believing in God/Higher Power. Tables such as this are especially helpful for readers who are interested in details of results. If details are numerous or long, the table can be placed in a report appendix.

CROSS-TABULATION TABLES. Cross-tabulation, or pivot, tables can be used to convey more complex information, as shown in table 5.4. These tables, in contrast to simpler tables such as those above, organize data from two different variables, juxtaposing them. In table 5.4, we can see whether respondents are using either alcohol or drugs after treatment or both together. Cross-tabulation tables convey a relatively large amount of data in a concise way. However, they may be more challenging for the reader to understand and may require more interpretation.

TABLE 5.4
Alcohol and Other Drug Use One Year after Treatment

		ALCOHOL USE		
		Abstinent	Moderate Drinking	Heavy Drinking
DRUG USE	Abstinent	55%	15%	10%
	Only as Prescribed	2%	1%	1%
	Using	2%	4%	10%

The proportions in table 5.4 add up to 100 percent; in other words, all the respondents fall into only one of the cells. In this case, alcohol use is compared with drug use. This comparison is particularly important in most alcohol and drug studies because abstinence from one does not imply abstinence from the other. In addition, it is not particularly helpful to know the frequencies of the two variables separately. For example, knowing that 59 percent of the respondents are abstinent from alcohol and 80 percent of the respondents are abstinent from other drugs gives no clue as to what proportion is abstinent overall. In this case, looking at the table, we can see that 57 percent of respondents are abstinent from both alcohol and drugs, if those who have used prescribed medications only as directed are included.

It is not necessary to repeat data already presented in tables in the narrative. Instead, use the narrative to highlight or summarize trends or provide overviews. The reader should be guided to the table for reference. For example, the report could contain the following sentences about table 5.1 on page 76: "As shown in table 5.1, women in Program X tended to be older than the men. They also had more years of education, were more likely to be employed, and had more dependent children. These gender differences reflect program changes in recent years, with new programs for professional women and young, unemployed men." This way, the narrative interprets the numbers and brings them to life.

Graphs

Some information is best conveyed in graphs or charts. This is particularly true when you want to draw the readers' eyes to important comparisons or show a trend line over time. Graphs include bar graphs, pie charts, line graphs, and scattergrams. They are easily produced using Excel or other software packages.

BAR GRAPHS. Bar graphs display proportions as blocks of color and can be especially helpful for showing comparisons between groups or time periods. Of course, the time frame of the comparisons must be equal. Figure 5.1 on page 81 is a bar graph showing the differences in legal, medical, and employment costs before and after treatment.

Note that bar graphs typically place labels along the x-axis, forming the horizontal bottom of the graph, and the y-axis, forming the vertical left side of the graph. A legend helps the reader understand the displayed information. In figure 5.1, the legend indicates which bars show pre-treatment data and which show post-treatment data.

FIGURE 5.1

Bar Graph

Legal, Health, and Employment Cost Comparisons
Pre-treatment and Twelve-Month Follow-Up

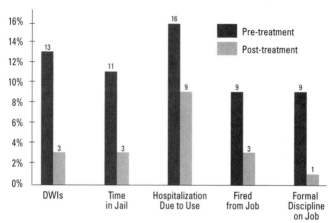

PIE CHARTS. Pie charts are useful for displaying results on one important variable. For example, figure 5.2 is a pie chart showing the distribution of primary drugs of choice in a group of patients before treatment.

FIGURE 5.2

Pie Chart

Primary Drugs of Choice in a Group of Patients Pre-treatment

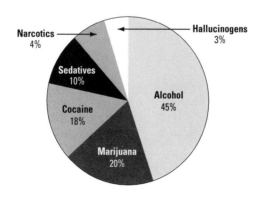

In figure 5.2, we see that the largest proportion of patients, 45 percent, describe their primary drug of choice as alcohol; 20 percent name marijuana; and so on, reading clockwise around the circle. Pie charts are useful for information where the parts total 100 percent, such as drug of choice or marital status. (All people—100 percent—can be classified as either married, divorced, widowed, or single never married.)

LINE GRAPHS. Reserve line graphs for continuous data, such as days, ages, or number of AA meetings. The line graphs in figures 5.3 below and 5.4 on page 83 belong to the general category of "survival analysis" because they show the cumulative proportion of people who succumb to an illness over time, in this case, alcohol or drug dependency.

Figure 5.3 shows hypothetical data for a population in which 80 percent of patients are still abstinent at the end of the first post-treatment month. Abstinence continues to drop each month until, by the end of the first year, the proportion

FIGURE 5.3
Line Graph

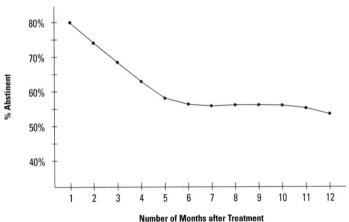

Abstinence by Months after Treatment

Number of Months after Treatment

of people who have maintained abstinence is 53 percent. Looking at the overall shape of the curve, we can see that the line steadily falls from the earliest days after discharge until about six months after discharge, when it seems to level out. In other words, we could say that the highest risk for relapse among this population is during the first six months. A goal of treatment might be to decrease the height slope of the line, that is, decrease the number of people who relapse at such high levels shortly after treatment.

FIGURE 5.4
Line Graph

Days to First Use after Treatment

Days to First Use

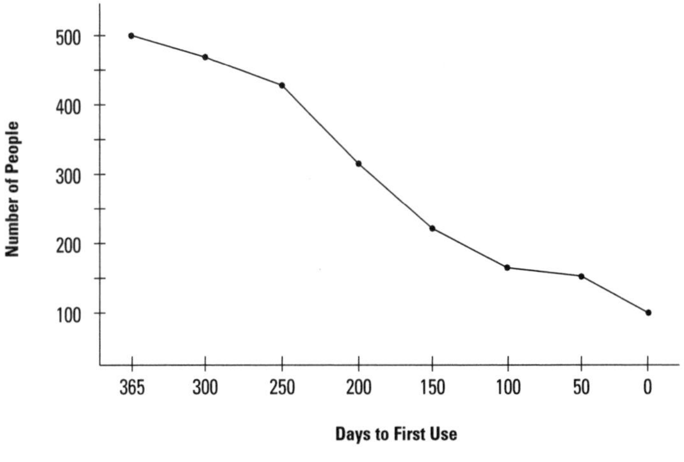

In figure 5.4, we see similar data presented as days to first use after treatment. This hypothetical graph shows the fall off in the number of people abstinent over time. We can see that 500 people (of about 2,500) maintained abstinence for the 365 days of follow-up. Another 450 maintained abstinence for 300 days, and so forth, until the final group of 100 people with zero days of abstinence, meaning they drank immediately upon discharge.

SCATTERGRAM. Finally, an interesting way to display responses on two variables is a scattergram. A scattergram can also be used to show how two different groups respond to the same variable. For example, you may want to compare self-report of abstinence with others' report of abstinence, as in the hypothetical scattergram in figure 5.5.

Figure 5.5 shows high agreement between parents and child. For example, looking at point A, in this case, the child reported he or she stayed abstinent for about 120 days, and the parent gave exactly the same report of 120 days. On the other hand, an outlier is shown by point B. In this case, the child reported he or she was abstinent for about 50 days, but the parent reported the period of abstinence to be longer, about 100 days. The measurement of agreement between two variables such as this is called a correlation. The correlation can range from -1.0 (responses that are totally opposite from

FIGURE 5.5

Scattergram

Comparison of Youth's Self-Report with
Parents' Report of Days Abstinent

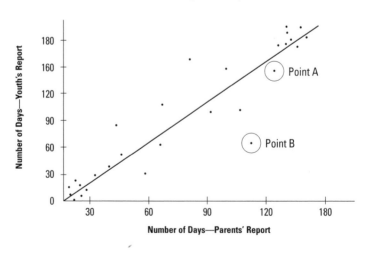

each other) to +1.0 (responses that are in total agreement with each other). A zero correlation indicates no pattern at all. Another way of telling correlation is by looking at the line drawn through the dots, indicating the best-fitting slope. A perfectly diagonal slope indicates perfect agreement between the responses of the two groups or items being compared.

Narrative

You cannot rely on tables and graphs alone to convey the information that the outcome study shows. Some of your readers will be uncomfortable with either graphs or tables and prefer narrative. This is true for many clinicians who think in terms of stories. The more the report reads like a story of a group of patients, the more they may be willing to "enter in" and absorb the information. The narrative is an important tool to point out the main points of the study and make the information easily digestible.

Surround your tables and graphs with well-written narrative and use appendices to add more tables, such as of the frequencies of all the variables. That way, as many readers as possible will be able to get the information they need from your report.

The executive summary is an important part of your report narrative. In the summary, you can lay out briefly and logically the conclusions and supporting evidence of the report. This allows your audience to get a quick overview and understanding of the information before they look at it closely.

Format

Generally, the format of the report follows the same structure as if it were to be published in a scholarly journal, though in a less formal or detailed way. The main sections are as follows:

- *Cover Page.* This contains the program name, the range of dates patients were in treatment, the study's author, and other staff who worked on the project.

- *Executive Summary*. This is a single page of main points, often in bulleted sentences.
- *Introduction*. This contains a description of the program and why the follow-up is being conducted.
- *Participants and Method*. This describes who is in the study, how they were contacted, what questions were asked, and the response rate.
- *Results*. This is the "meat" of the report, describing all the main findings. When possible, use comparisons over time or with other programs in order to address the "so-what" question.
- *Summary*. This is a narrative, reviewing the main findings and their clinical implications.
- *Appendix*. This contains simple frequencies of many of the items and other details of interest.

Observations about Writing a Report for External Audiences

All of what we've said about writing reports for internal audiences applies equally to writing reports for external audiences. However, when providing information to external audiences, you may want to add financial outcome indicators. You may also need to consider the issue of using the report for marketing purposes.

Adding Financial Outcome Indicators

Stakeholders who wonder if treatment is worthwhile want to know whether the negative and costly consequences of alcohol and drug dependency decrease after treatment. Even more importantly, they want to know if the decrease in costly consequences is large enough to justify the cost of treatment. The savings may apply to a funder, to a family, or to society at large. Legal, medical, and employment variables can all be converted to financial indicators, as shown in table 5.5 on page 87.

TABLE 5.5

Cost Indicators for Alcohol and Drug Treatment

Legal	Number of arrests Number of days in jail	Cost to society
Medical	Number of clinic visits Number of days in hospital Number of emergency room visits Number of ambulance calls Actual claim costs	Cost to provider, employer, individual, and/or society
Employment	Number of days missed Number of accidents Cost of workers comp claims	Cost to employer

There are two approaches to reporting cost-related items. The first is to convert each item to a dollar amount, using local average estimates of costs. For example, you may determine that a typical day in a hospital costs $800, an emergency room visit $1,500, or an arrest $5,000. These amounts are for illustration purposes only. If conversions are used, seek realistic numbers based on actual research or reports and be consistent in applying the same dollar amounts across participants and across time. The CALDATA study converted episodes of health and legal problems to estimated dollar amounts for the State of California and was able to demonstrate that for every dollar California spent on treatment, seven dollars were saved, primarily through reduced legal costs to society.[3]

The second approach is to use a bar graph to show the changes in the indicators before and after treatment, without assigning dollar amounts to the indicators. For example, Hazelden asked patients about the number of legal, health, and employment consequences before and after treatment and found significant decreases in the year after treatment. Figure 5.1 on page 81 displays these findings.

While using actual or estimated dollar amounts to reflect benefits of treatment might be most informative, good use of graphics can also present a compelling story.

Using a Report for Marketing

An internal report should generally not be used for marketing. It's better to write a different report for marketing, aimed more at external audiences. While preparing external reports is beyond the scope of this book, we should take time to consider the differences between an internal report and an external report and the value of making the outcome data widely available.

The internal report is best thought of as a general source report. Its goal is to educate internal stakeholders and improve treatment. At the same time, it's important to share your information more broadly. The more the addiction field discloses and explains its outcomes, the more people working in the field can learn from each other and better educate the public. Even if your results don't seem great, being open about them and what actions you are taking to improve outcomes help build trust.

You may find yourself in a position of using your outcomes to respond to media questions or add to a market piece. This can be an opportunity to educate an even wider audience about treatment outcomes, their complexity, and how they are measured. If you are in this position, make sure you disclose how the sample was selected, what the response rate was, and what outcomes you obtained across several domains of life including, of course, alcohol and drug use. While presenting the information simply without minimizing limitations or complexity, it can be worth the effort. By sharing your outcome study with a larger audience, you receive more feedback from a wider range of stakeholders and gain ideas about how to improve your outcome monitoring system.

6

Special Settings and Populations

We have discussed all the main elements that make up a naturalistic outcome study: how to decide what to measure in order to determine success; how to select and define variables; how to develop, test, and administer the questionnaire; how to analyze the data; and, finally, how to present the findings. This approach for collecting and reporting outcomes provides a solid foundation for any program. However, certain settings and populations demand modifications in the outcome study. In the following pages, we'll discuss some of these special situations and the important variations.

Corrections

As more people are being incarcerated for alcohol- and drug-related offenses, many prison systems have responded by incorporating treatment into the prison term. Corrections outcome studies are particularly difficult to conceptualize and carry out for several reasons.

- Prisoners may not be released after they have completed treatment, so the follow-up may need to be aimed at measuring inmates' adjustment and functioning in the prison system rather than out in society.

- Release dates from prison will vary. Consequently, it is difficult to set up standardized time frames for follow-up.

- Inmates may be particularly distrustful of promises of confidentiality and perceive they have much to lose if they disclose alcohol or drug use after treatment, whether still incarcerated or at home.

- Many prisoners may have difficulty reading.

- Inmates are a protected class, so special consent procedures must be followed. For example, the study may need to be reviewed by an Institutional Review Board, following specific guidelines. (See chapter 4 for information about IRBs.) It is also a good idea to get a certificate of confidentiality to add extra protection for confidentiality. (See www.nida.nih.gov/Funding/ConfidentialityFAQ.html.)

- Prison staff are often overloaded with numerous other responsibilities for documentation, so helping with an outcome study may be low on their priority lists.

Recommendations

Keep your outcome monitoring system as simple as possible for all involved. Use as much already-captured administrative data as possible for baseline and outcome results. For example, state records will show if a released prisoner has been rearrested and re-incarcerated. Even if you are unable to obtain good data on inmates' alcohol and drug use after treatment, you should be able to determine number of disciplinary episodes while in prison and arrest and incarceration rates after release. In some states, it may be possible to access parole officer's documentation after release and periodic urine-testing results. When you are able to get information directly from an inmate or parolee, rely more on interviews than on paper-and-pencil tests, or construct the questionnaires so that they can be completed either way.

Several good outcome studies of inmates have been completed. You might refer to these to gain a better understanding of the complexities involved and how to overcome them.[1]

Employee Assistance Programs (EAPs)

Employee assistance programs are developed and maintained on the premise that troubled employees who get help are better employees. Some companies are especially impressed if their employee assistance program can demonstrate that its services provide cost containment, if not cost benefit. Medical boards overseeing the licensing of physicians or pharmacists and the referral services within the legal profession serve purposes similar to those of an EAP.

At one time, most EAPs were internal to the companies they served and provided services only to that company. Now the trend has shifted. Most employee assistance programs are offered by independent contractors who provide referral and counseling services to a large number of companies of various sizes and types.

Most employees who seek help do so for emotional and family problems, and only a relatively small proportion go to the EAP for alcohol or drug problems. However, when alcohol or drug treatment is required, it is important for the EAP to be able to demonstrate effectiveness. This is especially true for cases where treatment is expensive, where the employee is in a safety-related position, such as an airline pilot, or where the employee is highly trained in a specialized area, such as a senior executive. In these cases, employers want to know that treatment works and will allow them to retain a good employee. Professional boards or groups, such as medical boards who refer physicians or nurses to treatment, also have high stakes in whether a person is able to return to functioning.

Recommendations

A key to success in evaluating outcomes in these situations is obtaining the patient's permission to seek information from the employer or board. This increases the credibility of your results. Once permission is obtained, ask the employer to supply information on variables such as number of days worked, number of unplanned absences, conflicts with co-workers and supervisors, accidents, and disciplinary actions. This information will help to compare employee performance before and after treatment.

Companies will also be interested in health care costs. As payers, they will want to know that their investment in their employee is worthwhile, both in terms of job factors and health care costs. The most accurate information is provided by actual claims data about each patient in the periods before and after treatment. Even if the information is obtainable only through patient self-report, health utilization data will help round out the picture of cost—and presumably savings—to the employer.

Health Maintenance Organizations (HMOs) and Managed Care Systems

Health maintenance organizations and related health care systems provide unique challenges for the researcher. Alcohol and drug services are embedded in a web of diverse services that may include detoxification, brief or intensive outpatient services, day hospital, residential or hospital inpatient programs, and a wide range of aftercare support groups. Assessment and referral may be done formally through a special department or more informally through a physician referral. Some services may be administered and provided directly within the HMO system, while others will be contracted out and provided by community services. In other words, there is no "captive audience" when it comes to alcohol- and drug-treatment patients; and, even when you believe you have a sample, participants may be hard to track within the health care system. It is harder to capture a finite treatment episode with a clear ending. The same staff may not follow a patient from intake to discharge, and documentation over a wide range of services and practitioners may be difficult to standardize.

There are advantages, though, to doing outcome research in health services: Typically, samples are large, and you may have access to a wealth of data such as medical problems and health services utilization that are unavailable to other researchers. In addition, as patients of a community provider, participants are likely to be living in a relatively geographically limited area, making them more available to follow-up by phone or even in-person.

Recommendations

Plan to capture multiple types of treatment, as well as length of treatment, in the data collection process for each participant. With this data, you may be able to group patients based on the types of services they receive. For example, some patients may receive only outpatient services, others may receive a combination of day hospital and outpatient, and still others may receive only a few physician visits with advice and support. Outcomes could be measured on overall length of time services are received and the combination of services received.

Keep track of all patients initially recruited as there will inevitably be attrition at various points of time, from pre-treatment through in-treatment. Some participants who drop out will fall into natural groups for comparison. For example, if you initially obtain permission to follow up 200 patients and 50 drop out even before beginning treatment, you have 50 people who did not receive treatment with whom to compare your results. At the same time, these two groups were self-selected rather than obtained by random assignment, so there may be some confounding variables such as motivation. If those who participate in treatment do better than those who did not, you may be able to obtain useful information to increase rates of patient retention.[2]

Medication

Medications are sometimes prescribed to help alleviate addiction. Medication studies look at the effect of these

93

medications on alcohol and drug treatment. Most typically, medication studies are double-blind; participants receive either a placebo or an active medication and neither they nor the person administering the medications knows which is being administered.

Medication studies also present special challenges to researchers. In traditional treatment settings, medications may not be the norm, and staff and patients may be unfamiliar with them. While attrition is always a problem in alcohol- and drug-treatment outcome research, it is especially frequent in medication studies. Patients sometimes change their minds about participation when they experience side effects, and they may drop out of treatment altogether. In these cases, if they have not received the full course of medication, it seems particularly misleading to attribute treatment failure to the medication. On the other hand, if the medication is helpful, we would expect fewer people to stop taking it. Finally, dose size is challenging to monitor. Some medications have increased effect with increased dosage, and this may vary by individual.

Recommendations

In medication studies, track all participants and their doses—both the actual size of individual pill dose and the length of time taken. Because attrition is expected, increase the sample size so you can compute the results for both the original sample (intent to treat) as well as a sample of individuals who received an adequate dose that would be expected to show a response. Measure craving by using standardized instruments, such as the Penn Alcohol Craving Scale[3] and the Obsessive Compulsive Drinking Scale.[4] Side-effect symptoms must also be collected and monitored. The most useful medication outcome studies, as is the case for traditional treatment programs, are those that demonstrate or test whether there is a treatment effect above and beyond normal treatment, and, most importantly, for whom. In addition, it is helpful to measure participant expectations as part of a medication outcome study. This may help you sort out drug effects and effects caused by patient expectations. For example, in a small study done on Naltrexone, the following items were incorporated into the baseline and follow-up questionnaires:

Which study medication do you think you are receiving? (check one)

1 Inactive (placebo)

2 Active (Naltrexone)

3 No opinion

Rate the effect of the study medication on your overall recovery. (check one)

1 No effect

2

3

4

5

6

7

8

9

10 The most important part of my recovery program

Questions such as these help the researcher and clinicians understand how patients incorporate medications into their overall recovery process.

Finally, even though the medication phase of treatment may only last a relatively short time, such as six to twelve weeks, plan to continue follow-up for at least one year. While medication may no longer be an "active ingredient" in the treatment process, it is reasonable to expect that patients who are successfully maintained on medication during the early recovery phases may benefit in the longer term from having had this increased "boost" during a critical time.

Adolescents

The biggest challenge in doing treatment outcome studies with adolescents is making contact with them and maintaining their interest in participating in the follow-up study. Adolescence and young adulthood can be a time for physical transitions, so many youth may be hard to locate. Many may go to a halfway house in another city after primary treatment and remain living in that city after discharge. Others go on to college or travel. Youth who are not doing well may live as transients, contacting even their parents only sporadically. Generally, when a youth is under the age of eighteen, parental consent is needed for inclusion in an outcome study. Finally, many items in standardized instruments used for outcome studies are developed on samples of adults and do not include typical milestones and barriers that youth face in early recovery.

Recommendations

When obtaining permission and location information from youth, ask for the location of their parents and permission to contact them as well. Youth are also more likely than other populations to use cell phones, so make sure to get cell phone numbers. Consider using e-mail follow-up methods, either to gather information or to arrange for a specific interview time. If possible, offer incentives in the form of gift certificates or other items such as phone cards.

Make sure to include items in the questionnaires that capture youth experiences. Instead of or in addition to employment variables, make sure to ask about school attendance, suspension, or disciplinary action. You may want to ask about grade point average. In one study of youth, Hazelden included the following item, which helped give a broader view of the young people's outcomes.

> In terms of where you think you should be at this stage in your life, as far as your work or career is concerned, where would you say you actually are?
>
> _____ (1) a good deal further ahead
>
> _____ (2) somewhat further ahead
>
> _____ (3) about where you should be
>
> _____ (4) somewhat behind
>
> _____ (5) a good bit behind

In addition, include items about friendships, not only regarding the number and sobriety of friends, but also how satisfied they are with the time, affection, understanding, and support they get from friends.

Women

While standard outcome questions work well for women, women also have experiences and needs that may be overlooked. For example, for many women relationships are especially important in the recovery process, both negatively, such as when they rejoin drug-abusing boyfriends, and positively, such as when they develop healthy friendships with men and women. During their active addiction, they may have formed relationships with men to obtain drugs and now need to practice building healthy sexual relationships. Relationships with children may also be especially important during women's recovery process. They may need to regain their children's trust, learn new parenting skills, and re-connect with children who may have been living in foster care or in relatives' homes. Women may have special issues in rebuilding self-esteem, learning to deal constructively with anger, overcoming depression, addressing eating disorders, and working through issues of physical or sexual abuse. In addition, some clinicians and patients anecdotally report changes in craving and alcohol or drug use during particular phases of the menstrual cycle. Finally, women may experience fewer legal consequences as a result of their alcohol or drug use, either because they are less likely than their male counterparts to incur legal consequences, or because they are less likely to be held accountable for them.[5]

Recommendations

Consider adding items to the outcome questionnaires that are likely to capture women's recovery or relapse experience. At a minimum, make sure that you include items about quality of relationships with friends, children, and spouse or partner, and general mental health functioning and treatment. If you are working with a women-only sample and have the ability to add more areas of inquiry, you may get useful information for program evaluation and improvement by exploring the relationship of relapse to menstrual cycle and social support, and by adding questions regarding dual disorders.

7

Some Landmark Studies

Researchers have been conducting outcome studies on alcohol and drug treatment programs for over fifty years. In recent years, interest in evaluating outcomes has grown markedly, and a number of excellent large-scale studies have been done that deserve special attention. Although the field of alcohol and drug treatment has not developed standardized procedures for outcome measurement, these recent studies can provide direction to anyone setting out to conduct an outcome study. In this chapter, we will do an overview of these studies. Familiarize yourself with at least some of them, especially ones that involve populations similar to yours. They can guide you in a variety of effective methods and may allow you to compare your results with results of other pertinent studies.

Bear in mind some important cautions, however, when you compare your results to those of others. First, it is difficult to know if the patient populations are comparable in severity. Studies may also differ greatly in the length and type of treatment provided, how patients were selected for the study, what the response rate was, and what criteria were used to measure outcomes. For example, one study might apply a strict methodology, including all consecutive admissions to treatment as the sample and tracking them rigorously to obtain an 85 percent response rate. Another study may only include patients who completed at least ten treatment sessions, with a 70 percent response rate. The latter program will probably report better results than the first program simply because it was studying a more favorable sample. This sample does not include early patient drop-outs and those who are hard to reach. People who drop out of treatment or are hard to reach generally have lower success rates. Researchers do not set out to create biased studies and reports, but they may be guided by a different philosophy or limited by resources. Therefore, it is extremely important to be aware of these differences when comparing outcomes. Similarly, be sure to use the same methodology and instruments of earlier studies conducted on populations like your own if you wish to compare outcomes.

Project MATCH

Project MATCH, a large-scale study funded in 1989 by the National Institute on Alcohol Abuse and Alcoholism (NIAAA), provides an illustration of an excellent study. It was an empirical study, using experimental methods to test differences between treatment approaches. The study included four elements critical to producing an exemplary empirical study: standardized instruments, random assignment, manualized therapy, and rigorous outcome monitoring. A researcher in a normal clinical setting can rarely reproduce all of these characteristics, but they are well worth emulating when possible.

Project MATCH was designed to determine what kind of treatment approach works best for what kind of person. Three therapy approaches were compared: cognitive behavioral therapy (CBT), motivational enhancement therapy (MET), and Twelve Step facilitation therapy (TSF). While this chapter cannot describe the entire project, including its methodology and findings, we will review the four significant elements noted above.

Standardized Instruments

The study spawned a spate of standardized instruments. A battery of instruments was given to each participant at baseline. These included the Structured Clinical Interview for

DSM-III (SCID), the Addiction Severity Index (ASI), Form 90, and several other tests to measure cognitive functioning, motivation, personality, and spirituality. Many were repeated during the follow-up phase. A description of the instruments and their psychometric properties can be found in a special issue of the *Journal of Studies on Alcohol*, supplement number 2, December 1994. More information about methodology and the overall research project can be found in a Web page created by the University of Connecticut, one of the participating research sites: www.commed.uchc.edu/match/default.htm.

Random Assignment

One problem in evaluating how well a treatment approach works is in removing any potential bias resulting from patients being referred to or choosing a particular form of treatment. For example, if a patient chooses a particular type of treatment and it proves to be effective, are the good results due to patient motivation or true effectiveness? Or, in another case, if low-income patients with few resources go to one type of treatment, and wealthier patients with many resources go to another, is any difference in results due to true differences in the treatment approaches or the inherent differences in the patients? Random assignment is used to make it equally likely that any patient is selected for any particular treatment type. Project MATCH used random assignment. All participants who met the criteria for the study were randomly assigned to one of the three therapy approaches. Most of the published research results are on the 952 people across five outpatient sites that participated in the study.

Manualized Therapy

Each of the three therapy approaches was fully described in a manual for a therapist to follow, session by session. These manuals are available through NIAAA at www.niaaa.nih. gov/publications/match.htm. Appendix 1 also contains an order blank. Even more important, monitoring was done throughout the study to make sure that each therapist was conducting therapy in accordance to the manual.

Rigorous Outcome Monitoring

The protocol called for participants to be contacted at frequent intervals, every three months during the first year following treatment. This procedure helped maintain contact with the participants, and the response rate was 90 percent. (Some people have pointed out that the frequency of follow-up may have inadvertently provided a form of case management, resulting in improved outcomes beyond what might have occurred with therapy alone.)

Outcomes were measured in many ways at various points in time. Some of the main findings at three years are shown in table 7.1.

TABLE 7.1
Outcomes of Project MATCH at Three Years

	THREE YEARS (past 90 days)		
	Mean Percent Days Abstinent	Drinks per Day of Drinking	Percent Abstinent
Cognitive Behavioral	nr	nr	24%
Motivational Enhancement	nr	nr	27%
Twelve Step Facilitation	nr	nr	36%*
Combined	69% / 56%**	5.62 / 5.96**	29.4%*

* p<.007 for TSF compared with the other two approaches

** results for total sample and non-abstainers only, respectively

nr = not reported

Drinking outcomes were measured in three ways: average percent of abstinent days, average number of drinks per day the person drank alcohol, and overall abstinence. These outcomes were based on the thirty-day window before the interview. Overall, researchers found that the best outcomes at three years were for the participants with higher severity or poorer social functioning at intake. They speculate that those with greater severity may have been more motivated to take advantage of treatment. In further analyses, researchers also found that better outcomes were associated with greater participation in Alcoholics Anonymous.[1]

Project MATCH actually had two subtypes of patients. One was the outpatient group. These patients participated in a certain number of outpatient therapy sessions over the course of about twelve weeks (twelve sessions of either cognitive behavioral therapy or Twelve Step therapy, or three to four sessions of motivational therapy). This is the subtype written about in most of the published articles. The other was an aftercare group. These were patients recruited to be in the study immediately after they had completed a much more intensive primary treatment in an overnight or day hospital setting. So, for these people their outpatient therapy was after treatment, in other words, aftercare. Researchers found that participants who had residential or day treatment plus aftercare in MATCH had better outcomes than participants who had just outpatient treatment through MATCH, with about 10 percent more abstinent days. This suggests that people who are involved in professional counseling following treatment have better outcomes.[2]

The Veterans Administration (VA) Studies

The Veterans Administration conducted a national outcome study of over 3,500 patients in fifteen VA hospitals across the country in 1997.[3] These facilities varied in the types of treatment approaches they used. Some used a cognitive behavioral therapy (CBT) approach, some used a form of treatment based on the Twelve Steps, and still others used an approach combining CBT and Twelve Step.

Unlike Project MATCH, the VA hospitals study was a naturalistic study, the type that studies the real-world environment but exerts less control of variables. Both the VA hospitals study and Project MATCH found significant improvements with treatment. They also found few differences in success rates between treatment approaches; but, when there were, they tended to favor the Twelve Step approach. As in Project MATCH, there was little evidence in the VA study to support the idea that matching patients to certain treatments based on their characteristics produces better outcomes. That is, overall, no major findings help us to understand what kind of treatment approach works best for whom. Finally, in both studies, patients who continued their recovery process by participating in professional counseling or AA attendance did better than those who did not.

The VA hospitals study compared the three treatment approaches used in VA facilities.[4] A summary of findings is shown in table 7.2 on page 105.

The researchers looked at outcomes in various ways. Participants were categorized as "abstinent" if they had used no alcohol or illicit drugs in the three months prior to the follow-up interview. Participants were categorized as "in remission" if they were drinking no more than 3 ounces of alcohol on a usual drinking day, were not using illicit drugs, and had no problems resulting from alcohol or drug use during the three-month time frame prior to the follow-up interview. As shown in table 7.2, abstinence ranged from about 19 percent to 26 percent, and remission ranged from about 23 percent to 30 percent. At outcome, about one-fifth were drinking at levels that met criteria for alcohol dependence; in other words, their use was problematic.

Patients in all three treatment settings improved on drinking-related psychological and psychosocial measures. The researchers did additional analyses and found that people with dual disorders did as well as people without dual disorders in terms of their alcohol use, but not as well in the areas of psychological functioning and employment. This was particularly true for people with psychotic and anxiety/depressive symptoms.

TABLE 7.2
Vererans Administration Study Results

RESULTS	COGNITIVE BEHAVIORAL (CB)	TWELVE STEP	COMBINATION CB and TWELVE STEP
% remission	24.1	29.5	22.5
% abstinent	18.5	25.5*	19.3
Mean alcohol consumption (oz.) per drinking day	3.97	3.68	4.19
% alcohol dependence	19.4	17.3	23.0
% without substance use problems	27.4	30.9	23.7
% depression	58.7	56.1	59.5
% anxiety	50.8	51.4	53.4
% w/no arrests	75.6	78.8	80.8
% employed	39.1*	43.4*	31.9
% not in jail or homeless	91.2	94.1	93.3

* Indicates methods for which outcomes were significantly greater than the comparison methods

A Multistudy Review

William Miller, a researcher at the University of New Mexico, reviewed seven studies to answer the question "How effective is alcoholism treatment in the United States?"[5] He used only outcome studies that were multisite, that followed patients for at least one year, and that obtained at least a 60 percent follow-up rate. Project MATCH and the VA hospitals study, both discussed above, met these criteria and were included in his review. For Project MATCH, he used both the outpatient group and the aftercare group.

Miller used the VA study described above, labeled VA Study 3 in table 7.3 on page 107. For his review, he combined the CBT and Twelve-Step groups since there were no significant differences overall between them. Miller also found two other VA studies that met his criteria, labeled VA Study 1 and VA Study 2 in table 7.3. VA Study 1 (1986) compared patients who were on disulfrum (or antabuse) and those who were not. At outcome, there were no significant differences between these two groups, so they could be combined into one group. Similarly, VA Study 2 (1989) compared patients on lithium with those who were not, and again found no differences at outcome, so those groups could also be combined.

To round out his review, Miller included the Relapse Replication and Extension Project (RREP),[6] which followed patients from three treatment programs, and the RAND project,[7] which followed patients from eight sites.

Miller sifted through the results of all the studies to find outcomes in two domains: alcohol/drug use in terms of abstinence and life improvement. Measurement of life improvement varied across studies. The Drinker Inventory of Consequences (DrInC) was used in the Project MATCH studies as a measure of life improvement. In two of the VA studies, the best indicator was unemployment; in another, the Addiction Severity Index (ASI) was used. A summary of Miller's findings is provided in table 7.3.

TABLE 7.3

Miller's Review of Seven Outcome Studies

STUDY	TREATMENT	SAMPLE	ABSTINENCE RATE	LIFE IMPROVEMENT
MATCH outpatient, 1997	Outpatient	952	19.0%	46.7% improvement in Drinker Inventory of Consequences
MATCH aftercare, 1997	Outpatient after residential or day hospital	774	35.0%	59.5% improvement in Drinker Inventory of Consequences
VA Study 1, 1986	Inpatient or out-patient primary plus one year outpatient	605	19.2%	12.6% decrease in unemployment
VA Study 2, 1989	30-day inpatient plus one year outpatient and AA	457	33.1%	68.7% improvement in Alcohol Severity Index
VA Study 3, 1997	Inpatient	3698	20.8%	41.0% decrease in unemployment
RREP Project, 1996	Varied	563	25.5%	nr
RAND, 1978	Varied	1340	16.7%	63.3% decrease of those with conse-quences or symptoms
Total		**8389**	**24.1%** (average)	

In addition to the main findings shown in table 7.3, Miller found that a small proportion, about 10 percent, seemed to be drinking moderately or without problems. Of those who were drinking, there were large reductions in frequency of drinking. For example, before treatment, these patients were drinking on 63 percent of the days; after treatment, they were drinking on 25 percent of the days. On days they drank before treatment, they drank an average of seventy-seven drinks per week; this fell to an average of ten drinks per week after treatment. Drinking-related problems decreased by 60 percent. Overall, Miller concluded, after one year of treatment, about one-third of patients will be doing well, and another one-third will be substantially improved. He points out that these outcomes are excellent when compared with outcomes of other chronic diseases.

Minnesota Treatment Outcome Study

The studies we have looked at thus far have been national studies. We'll look now at a large-scale study done within one state system, Minnesota.[8] The Minnesota treatment outcome study is a unique study in that the researchers were able to obtain good ASI outcome data on patients discharged from a wide range of treatment programs. In this study, outcomes of 36,770 adult outpatients, 1,283 adult inpatients, 214 adolescent outpatients, and 173 adolescent inpatients treated in 231 adult treatment programs and 49 adolescent programs were followed at six months post-treatment. The response rate was good: Researchers were able to locate 83.5 percent of the adolescents and 64.4 percent of the adults. At six months, they found that 59.8 percent of the adult inpatients, 63.8 percent of the adult outpatients, and 21.4 percent of the adolescents were abstinent.

Indicators of impairment dropped significantly across several different areas. When comparing outpatient and inpatient, the researchers found similar results for patients with lower levels of severity. At higher levels of severity, patients did better in inpatient treatment. Good outcome for adults was associated with treatment completion and a history of close relationships. Good outcome for adolescents was associated with treatment completion, parental monitoring, legal coercion, and being female. Adolescents who were treated in an all-adolescent specialty program had higher abstinence rates than those treated in a mixed adult-adolescent program: 25.1 percent versus 15.0 percent. Women in specialty programs tended to have more severe problems and were less likely to complete treatment. But, even with those factors considered, abstinence rates were good; 59.0 percent in the specialty programs versus 61.7 percent in the mixed-gender programs.

Patricia Harrison and Steve Asche also looked more carefully at the results of patients who participated in aftercare following treatment. Specifically, they looked at professionally led aftercare groups and peer-led aftercare groups, most typically AA, and found that patients who participated in both did best. Among treatment completers with no involvement in aftercare, abstinence rates were 53.7 percent for adults and 15.8 percent for adolescents. For those who participated in either formal aftercare or AA, abstinence rates were 73.1 percent for adults and 37.5 percent for adolescents. Finally, for those who participated in both aftercare and AA, abstinence rates were 82.5 percent and 42.3 percent, respectively, for adults and adolescents. This study provides good information about the importance of continuing recovery activities after formal treatment.

Private Treatment Program Study

Most published outcome results are from publicly funded treatment programs, such as those done through the VA or through other federally funded research projects. A unique study was done by another group of researchers on private treatment programs, two of which were inpatient and two outpatient.[9] They reported their results both in terms of abstinence as well as by comparing ASI scores. The outcomes they found at six months after treatment are shown in table 7.4 on page 110.

As shown, a larger proportion of participants were abstinent from alcohol or drugs at the time of follow-up, six months after treatment, and working at least thirty hours a week. There were significant improvements in most areas from time of treatment entry to follow-up. There were no significant differences in outcomes between the two modalities, inpatient and outpatient. However, many of the differences between outpatient program 1 and outpatient program 2 were significant. There were also significant differences between the two inpatient programs. Among other things, this study provides good basic information about intake and outcome status of patients in terms of basic frequencies of problems as well as ASI scores.

TABLE 7.4

McLellan et al. Outcomes of Private Treatment Centers

	OUTPATIENT		INPATIENT		TOTAL PROGRAM
	PROGRAM 1	PROGRAM 2	PROGRAM 1	PROGRAM 2	
Abstinent from alcohol	51%	45%	78%	63%	59%
Abstinent from drugs	80%	71%	87%	98%	84%
Working more than 30 hours a week	80%	72%	74%	83%	77%

Abstinence based on use in past 30 days before interview.

National Databases of Treatment Outcomes

Two national, naturalistic large-scale treatment outcome studies were conducted in the 1990s. In both cases, researchers aggregated and analyzed data from patients treated in community-based treatment and followed up one year after treatment.

Drug Abuse Treatment Outcome Study (DATOS)

The Drug Abuse Treatment Outcome Study (DATOS) contacted over 4,000 patients across 76 treatment programs.

Researchers achieved a response rate of 62 percent, contacting 2,966 patients. The sample was analyzed in four different treatment types, as shown in table 7.5.

These data are somewhat difficult to interpret as the researchers did not analyze and report the outcomes in terms of abstinence. Overall, they found 50 percent reductions in drug use, illegal activities, and psychological distress, though there were differences across treatment types. The best outcomes were associated with longer length of stay and being in treatment for the first time. Results are available at www.datos.org.

TABLE 7.5

DATOS Outcomes

TREATMENT TYPE	N	SUBSTANCE USE OUTCOME	FUNCTIONING OUTCOME
Long-term Residential (4 months to 2 years)	676	67% drop in number of weekly cocaine users, 53% decline in heavy drinkers	Unemployment dropped 13%, suicide ideation dropped 46%, illegal activity dropped 61%. Drop from 77% to 35% being in jail. Arrests decreased from 56% to 31%.
Short-term Inpatient (up to 30 days)	799	69% drop in weekly cocaine users, 63% drop in weekly marijuana users, 58% decline in number of heavy drinkers	No change in unemployment, suicidal ideation fell by 48%, illegal activity dropped 58%. Jail decreased from 49% to 20% and those with any arrests decreased from 26% to 20%.
Outpatient Drug-free (3 to 6+ months)	764	57% drop in weekly cocaine users, 64% reduction in weekly marijuana users, 52% drop in heavy drinkers	Unemployment dropped 7%, suicidal ideation dropped 42%, and illegal activity dropped 36%.
Outpatient Methadone (2+ years)	727	69% drop in weekly heroin use, 48% decline in weekly cocaine use	Illegal activity decreased 52%. Percent jailed dropped from 63% one year before treatment to 21% during year after treatment.

National Treatment Improvement Evaluation Study (NTIES)

A similar national study called the National Treatment Improvement Evaluation Study (NTIES) was done by aggregating data from 4,411 patients across 71 treatment programs funded by the Center for Substance Abuse Treatment. One year after treatment, the researchers were able to contact 3,205 patients, for a response rate of 73 percent. Their results are shown in table 7.6. The researchers found the best outcomes associated with longer length of stay in each modality (65 percent with longer stays versus 57 percent with shorter stays) and with higher patient satisfaction (67 percent of those who were highly satisfied with treatment versus 51 percent reporting low satisfaction). Full results are available at neds.calib.com.

These studies show the wide range of methods used to measure outcomes, and the results obtained. The field of alcohol and drug treatment has not agreed on one standard methodology and set of instruments for follow-up studies, which makes comparisons for the sake of learning and

TABLE 7.6

NTIES Treatment Outcomes

	ABSTINENCE*
Overall (N=3205)	32%
Short-term residential (mean LOS=50 days)	28%
Long-term residential (mean LOS=107 days)	37%
Methadone outpatient (mean LOS=302 days)	16%
Non-methadone outpatient (mean LOS=127 days)	35%
Correctional (mean LOS=70 days)	32%

* abstinence defined as using less than 5 times in the last 30 days

LOS = length of stay

improvement difficult. Whatever outcome approach you choose to take, familiarize yourself with at least some of the studies that involve populations similar to yours. By using some of their methodology and measurement methods, you will be in a better position to compare your outcomes with theirs. In doing so, you may discover ways in which your program has strengths, and ways in which it could improve.

>

8

New Directions

Historically, outcome evaluation studies have been done for two main reasons: for internal use so administrators could make sure their programs were working well, and for external audiences to demonstrate treatment effectiveness. The purposes were quite insular; the information might be to demonstrate to accrediting bodies that evaluation was taking place, or to contractors to demonstrate that treatment works. Moving into the future, however, outcome monitoring systems and results are playing a much more integral role in organizational functioning. In this chapter, we will look at ways that organizations can leverage outcome systems to greater benefit.

Challenging Program Philosophy

Outcome studies that assume that there are varied definitions of success report a range of indicators clearly, unequivocally, and broadly enough to reflect the subtleties of program philosophy. This allows program administrators and clinicians to struggle with and hone their own definitions of their program's philosophy.

As we saw in chapter 2, outcomes (specifically abstinence) can be measured in a myriad of ways. A program's goal for complete and continuous abstinence for patients can remain the key indicator of program success; but what about patients who relapse once, briefly, and return to abstinence and commit themselves even more earnestly to abstinence and a program of recovery? These people may be struggling, but they are struggling in the right direction. Unfortunately, with the definition of success limited to total continuous abstinence, this person will be missed and considered a treatment failure. On the other hand, if a limited number of "days of use" are "allowed" in the success category, some adherents to the program philosophy may see a conflicting message: "Our goal for you is to remain continuously abstinent, but if you don't, we'll still count you as a success." Recovery is not a simple process, and neither is the measurement of it. However, the more the complexity is measured, the better the outcome study is.

Similarly, as we go into the future, some outcome studies are shifting the way they look at the importance of overall functioning. It is entirely possible for individuals to attain abstinence, but have a relatively poor quality of life. Nothing has changed in their lives but their use of a substance. Some programs, such as Twelve Step programs, differentiate between recovery and abstinence. People may be abstaining, but they may not be in recovery. That is, they may still be unhappy and self-centered and living chaotic lifestyles. Abstinence is a necessary but insufficient condition for treatment success.

How can results be reported in a way that is clear and unequivocal, yet broad enough to reflect the subtleties of program philosophy? The best solution is to measure abstinence and functioning in very detailed, specific ways, so that they can be reported in several ways. This solution allows readers to take away the information they need to judge treatment effectiveness. For example, using Form 90, researchers can report outcomes in any of the following ways:

- Average percent of days drinking
- Average amount of drinks per drinking day
- Average percent of days using drugs
- Average percent of days using alcohol or drugs

- Proportion abstinent from alcohol
- Proportion abstinent from any of several categories of drugs
- Proportion maintaining total abstinence from alcohol and drugs
- Days to first use of any substance after treatment
- Days since any use of any substance (from time of follow-up contact)
- Proportion using one day
- Proportion using two days
- Proportion using less than any number of days
- Proportion with one episode only, under three (or any selected number of) days
- Proportion using less than 3 ounces/day
- Proportion using (any amount or any length of time) with or without problems

These various indicators allow readers to choose and determine what best defines their idea of success. Reporting outcomes in numerous ways also makes comparisons easier across a wide range of other studies.

In addition to presenting various permutations of abstinence, as above, a simple way of presenting outcomes is to use a composite indicator, as shown in table 8.1.[1]

TABLE 8.1

Composite Outcomes

| | | ALCOHOL/DRUG USE STATUS | |
		Positive	Negative
FUNCTIONING OR PROBLEM STATUS	Positive	++, no use, no problems	-+, used, no problems
	Negative	+-, no use, with problems	- -, used, with problems

Viewed in a dichotomous way, those in the left (positive) column used no alcohol or drugs and so could be viewed as treatment successes while those in the right (negative) column did use alcohol or drugs and could be viewed as treatment failures. A researcher could choose to divide all participants into two categories called "abstinent" and "non-abstinent." However, the details in this grid more clearly show outcomes and allow the reader to analyze success and failure. While everyone would agree that those in the upper-left quadrant are treatment successes, and those in the lower-right quadrant are treatment failures, what about those in the other two quadrants? Those in the upper-right quadrant need to be analyzed more carefully. Researchers at Hazelden, for example, typically find that a large portion of people who relapse actually have attained abstinence at the time of the follow-up call, but had used earlier.

In summary, it is best if the outcome researcher does not define success, but instead reports the information in varied ways so that others can apply the information to their own needs. If the facts are well supplied, then the program administrators and clinicians are the ones who can and should define success in their programs.

Broadening the Benchmarks

Alcohol and drug dependence is a chronic disease. Outcome studies that allow alcohol and drug treatment outcomes to be compared with other chronic diseases enable program staff to put their treatment outcomes into context and learn from other disease management approaches. If alcohol and drug treatment outcome results seem discouraging, it is enlightening to compare them with outcomes of other chronic diseases, an approach taken by McLellan and his associates.[2]

Diabetes, hypertension, and asthma, for instance, are similar to alcohol and drug dependency. They all have genetic and environmental contributory causes; treatment is a combination of medical and psychosocial applications, with emphasis on lifestyle changes and adaptation to the condition; and there is no cure. Treatment success for these conditions can be judged by two factors: patient's adherence to the treatment regimen and remission of symptoms.

In the best of circumstances, success rates in the alcohol/drug treatment field generally range between 40 and 60 percent. Studies often show that one-third do very well, one-third are doing better but are not fully into recovery, and one-third show no improvement or are worse.[3] Reviewing the outcome literature for diabetes, hypertension, and asthma, McLellan and his colleagues found that patient compliance with the physician's orders generally ranged between 30 percent and 60 percent.[4] In other words, a large percentage did not take medications as prescribed nor adhere to diet or behavioral changes necessary to sustain remission. Looking at remission, the researchers found that 30 percent to 50 percent of patients with hypertension, asthma, or diabetes needed re-treatment within a year to reestablish remission. This is very analogous to what is sometimes perceived as the "revolving door" in alcohol and drug dependency treatment, which is frustrating to clinicians, funders, and the general public alike. Surprisingly, the situation is very similar for other chronic illnesses. What is the lesson? We need to consider alcohol/drug treatment outcomes in the context of a chronic disease and learn from other disease management approaches.

Examining the Process of Recovery

Another new direction in outcome studies is to measure recovery in phases—as a process, rather than as a presumed end product. This allows program staff to understand the process itself better, what propels recovery, and what derails it. Short-term outcomes can also more legitimately be claimed as the responsibility of the treatment program. Finally, analyzing phases or taking "snapshots" during or soon after recovery also allows the outcome study to contribute to case management or disease management and to quality improvement initiatives.

Typically, the alcohol and drug treatment field has measured outcomes in terms of success at some distant point from treatment, such as six months or one year. Some might argue that the best studies measure outcomes even farther down the road, at three, five, or even ten years. Another school of thought suggests, counterintuitively perhaps, that the best measures of outcome are much shorter, one to three months after treatment or, even more surprising, during the treatment process itself. The thinking behind this is twofold. First, while measurement during the treatment process or early recovery may not reveal whether treatment will be successful in helping the patient to maintain lifelong abstinence and improved quality of life, it does indicate whether the patient is on the right path and proceeding at a reasonable pace.

Measuring outcomes during or shortly after treatment also gives a greater guarantee that the success being seen is attributable to the treatment program. The farther out we go in time, the less responsibility for results—good or bad—a treatment program can take for any individual's course of treatment. During treatment, it is the program's responsibility to ensure that patients are receiving the care and counseling that will help them meet prescribed treatment goals. If they are not, modifications can be made in the treatment plan, a patient's stay can be extended, further assessments can be done, or other actions can be taken. One month after treatment, a program may still have quite a bit of influence as to whether a patient attends and participates in an AA group. While the patient may not be physically in the treatment program, strong case management services can be extended to the patient and his or her family to help them bridge whatever leap may exist between the support and structure of treatment and the less intensive services in the community. In these ways, treatment can assume some responsibility for the patient's ability to continue on the path of recovery.

However, as weeks and months go by, the treatment episode has less impact on the patient as he or she is subjected to greater environmental influences. By the time one year elapses, for example, patients may be exposed to numerous random events such as the death of a significant other, a job loss, or a geographical move that are not at all related to their own recovery behaviors. These will unevenly challenge the study sample. While ideally patients have learned to cope with unexpected negative events, the treatment program has no control over their occurrence. Patients might also enter another treatment program altogether, and the success that the original treatment program may be claiming one year after treatment may actually be a direct result of a second treatment that occurred during the tenth month.

This is not to say that long-term outcomes should be abandoned; instead, treatment programs need to work harder to measure and understand how shorter-term outcomes lead to the longer-term outcomes. In other words, we need to identify milestones of recovery and measure patients' progress in doing the next right thing on that pathway.

As outcome measurement becomes more common in alcohol and drug treatment programs, we will begin to see better integration of outcome measurement with quality-of-life improvement initiatives. Outcome measurement and quality improvement have somewhat different methods and goals, and both sides sometimes miss important ways they can work together. Outcome researchers would do well to coordinate efforts with quality measurement staff to ensure that common goals and measurement systems increase synergy and ultimately improve outcomes.

As noted, outcome research historically has been more concerned with measuring and evaluating the end points of a process (treatment). Quality initiatives have focused on measuring and changing processes, using specific tools. For example, at Hazelden, treatment is conceptualized as consisting of five key processes, as shown in table 8.2.

TABLE 8.2

Hazelden's Five Main Treatment Processes

PROCESS	WHAT HAPPENS WHEN PROCESS GOES WELL	HOW MEASURED
Pre-entry	Patient is appropriate for admission.	Staff rating on appropriateness of admission.
Intake	Patient is stable.	Documentation of medical and psychological status.
Assessment	Patient's problems are understood; nothing missed; assessment is thorough, accurate.	Verification of problem identification by clinical case review.
Care	Patient receives individualized treatment plan, makes good progress.	Clinical case review. Patient satisfaction; treatment completed with staff approval.
Continuing Care	Patient is linked with appropriate community/ongoing care.	Patient is attending recommended continuing care program/activities.

The ultimate outcome of all five processes is abstinence and improved psychosocial functioning. If the system, that is, the group of processes, is working well, then the successful completion of one process leads to a good beginning on the next process. For example, if patients fully meet all admission criteria, then they are likely to be relatively easily stabilized and oriented during the intake process. If intake goes smoothly, then they are likely to be forthcoming with information during the assessment process. If the assessment process goes well, a good treatment plan will be developed that the patient can accomplish. Finally, if a solid treatment plan is successfully completed, patients are apt to be more willing and able to continue their care plan. In other words, the end point of each process is a mini-outcome. The overall outcome, abstinence and improved psychosocial functioning, is the meta-outcome, the result of successful processes.

Quality measurement differs from traditional outcome research in several ways. First, quality measurement uses different tools and statistical methods to analyze data, including control charts. Control charts are simply line graphs of results over time, with standard deviations indicated on the chart. Second, quality measurement projects typically use repeated small samples to look for trends rather than a single aggregate large sample. Third, quality improvement studies are often designed to be quick, so that several improvements can be tried sequentially, and processes refined. These are called "rapid-cycle" studies.

While there are differences in the methods and goals of outcome measurement and quality measurement, they can work synergistically to benefit each other.

Automated Systems

Automated data collection is growing, enabling outcome researchers to provide information much sooner. This allows frequent analysis and reporting and gives information to administrators and program staff while they can still use it for the patients in question.

Traditionally, outcome data are collected using paper-and-pencil questionnaires and results are entered manually into a computer database. New technology is streamlining the process. For example, data can be entered by keyboard or touch screen directly by staff or by patients using a computer station. Ideally, the outcome data needs are integrated into clinical needs, resulting in a single, automated medical record and database. Questionnaires that are not in the system-wide database can be formatted on forms, which can be scanned into the computer and added to a patient's database. E-mails can be sent to patients at follow-up periods, linking the patient to a Web-based questionnaire where responses are automatically added to the database. The more flexible and integrated an outcome monitoring system is, the more likely it is to provide valuable data over many years.

Efforts in the field of outcome research are expanding and broadening the opportunities to provide useful information about treatment—what's working and what isn't. Exciting new developments are taking place that let researchers refine their work and give administrators, clinicians, and other stakeholders important information for improving the treatment process.

Outcomes can be measured and used to enhance treatment effectiveness, whether a program is simple or complex, has many resources or none. At the most basic level, an attempt can be made using the tools in this book to contact all patients at least once and report their data in simple tables and charts. At a more complex level, patients can be contacted repeatedly over time by e-mail and telephone, and their results displayed in trend reports and survival analysis graphs. The most critical factor is that, whatever methods are chosen, consistency and organization are maintained. While it may seem overwhelming to begin an outcome monitoring project, remember you don't have to achieve perfection at once. Enhancements can be added. The key is to have a solid system of good information, with a clear, frequent reporting system built in. With this in place, stakeholders will be able to use the information and provide good recommendations for improvements and additional needs. Having a stable outcome monitoring system in place will provide consistent, helpful information for years to come.

➤

Appendixes

APPENDIX 1

Ordering Information for NIAAA Manuals

To order the Project MATCH manuals, print and fill out the form below and mail to:

National Institute on Alcohol Abuse and Alcoholism
Publications Distribution Center
P.O. Box 10686
Rockville, MD 20849-0686

Cost: Volumes 1 through 7—$5.00 per copy
(includes handling and shipping)
Volume 8—Free

-- mail this portion --

Please fill in the number of copies you are requesting:

_____ Volume 1. *Twelve Step Facilitation Therapy Manual*

_____ Volume 2. *Motivational Enhancement Therapy Manual*

_____ Volume 3. *Cognitive-Behavioral Coping Skills Therapy Manual*

_____ Volume 4. *The Drinker Inventory of Consequences (DrInC)*

_____ Volume 5. *Form 90: A Structured Assessment Interview for Drinking and Related Behaviors*

_____ Volume 6. *Improving Compliance with Alcoholism Treatment*

_____ Volume 7. *Strategies for Facilitating Protocol Compliance in Alcoholism Treatment Research*

_____ Volume 8. *Project MATCH Hypotheses: Results and Causal Chain Analyses*

Total cost of volumes ordered	$ _____
Shipping and handling (Add 25% outside the continental U.S.)	$ _____
Total amount enclosed	$ _____

continued on other side

For organizations paying by check,
the NIAAA Federal ID No. is: 52-08-58115

Please choose method of payment:

_____ Check or money order payable to
NIAAA Publications Distribution Center/CSR, Inc.

_____ VISA   _____ MasterCard

_/

Expiration date: _____

Signature: _____

Cardholder's name: _____
PLEASE PRINT

Items requested will be shipped to:

_____
Name (M.D., Ph.D., R.N., Other)

_____
Organization

_____
Street, City, State, ZIP Code

_____
Telephone Number

_____
E-mail Address

Source for Volume 4, The Drinker Inventory of Consequences (DrInC): NIH Pub. No. 95-3911. 1995 (94 pp.).

Source for Volume 5, Form 90: A Structured Assessment Interview for Drinking and Related Behaviors Test Manual: NIH Pub. No. 96-4004. 1996 (123 pp.).

Addiction Severity Index, Fifth Edition
Clinical/Training Version

A. Thomas McLellan, Ph.D.
Kimberly A. Pukstas
Tara L. Deifenderfer

• • •

Remember: This is an interview, not a test.

*Item numbers circled are to be asked at follow-up.
Items with an asterisk are cumulative and should be
rephrased at follow-up.*

• • •

INTRODUCING THE ASI: Introduce and explain the seven potential problem areas: Medical, Employment/Support Status, Alcohol, Drug, Legal, Family/Social, and Psychiatric. All clients receive this same *standard* interview. All information gathered is *confidential;* explain what that means in your facility; who has access to the information and the process for the release of information.

There are *two time periods* we will discuss:
1. The past 30 days
2. Lifetime

Patient Rating Scale:

Patient input is important. For each area, I will ask you to use this scale to let me know how bothered you have been by any problems in each section. I will also ask you how important treatment is for you for the area being discussed.

The scale is:
> 0 - Not at all
> 1 - Slightly
> 2 - Moderately
> 3 - Considerably
> 4 - Extremely

Inform the client that he/she has the right to refuse to answer any question. If the client is uncomfortable or feels it is too personal or painful to give an answer, instruct the client not to answer. Explain the benefits and advantages of answering as many questions as possible in terms of developing a comprehensive and effective treatment plan to help them.

Please try not to give inaccurate information!

• • •

INTERVIEWER INSTRUCTIONS:

1. Leave no blanks.
2. Make plenty of Comments (if another person reads this ASI, they should have a relatively complete picture of the client's perceptions of his/her problems).
3. X = Question not answered. N = Question not applicable.
4. Terminate interview if client misrepresents two or more sections.
5. When noting comments, please write the question number.

Half Time Rule: If a question asks the number of months, round up periods of 14 days or more to 1 month. Round up 6 months or more to 1 year.

Confidence Ratings:

• Last two items in each section.
• Do not over-interpret.
• Denial does not warrant misrepresentation.
• Misrepresentation = overt contradiction in information.

Probe, cross-check and make plenty of comments!

• • •

HOLLINGSHEAD CATEGORIES:

1. Higher execs, major professionals, owners of large businesses.
2. Business managers if medium sized businesses, lesser professions, i.e., nurses, opticians, pharmacists, social workers, teachers.
3. Administrative personnel, managers, minor professionals, owners/ proprietors of small businesses, i.e., bakery, car dealership, engraving business, plumbing business, florist, decorator, actor, reporter, travel agent.
4. Clerical and sales, technicians, small businesses (bank teller, book-keeper, clerk, draftsperson, timekeeper, secretary).

5. Skilled manual—usually having had training (baker, barber, brake-person, chef, electrician, fireperson, lineperson, machinist, mechanic, paperhanger, painter, repairperson, tailor, welder, policeperson, plumber).

6. Semi-skilled (hospital aide, painter, bartender, bus driver, cutter, cook, drill press, garage guard, checker, waiter, spot welder, machine operator).

7. Unskilled (attendant, janitor, construction helper, unspecified labor, porter, *including unemployed*).

8. Homemaker.

9. Student, disabled, no occupation.

• • •

LIST OF COMMONLY USED DRUGS:

Alcohol:	Beer, wine, liquor
Methadone:	Dolophine, LAAM
Opiates:	Pain killers = Morphine, Diluaudid, Demerol, Percocet, Darvon, Talwin, Codeine, Tylenol 2, 3, 4, Robitussin, Fentanyl
Barbiturates:	Nembutal, Seconal, Tuinol, Amytal, Pentobarbital, Secobarbital, Phenobarbital, Fiorinol
Sed/Hyp/Tranq:	Benzodiazepines = Valium, Librium, Ativan, Serax, Tranxene, Xanax, Miltown Other = ChloralHydrate (Noctex), Quaaludes, Dalmane, Halcion
Cocaine:	Cocaine Crystal, Free-Base Cocaine or "Crack," and "Rock Cocaine"
Amphetamines:	Monster, Crank, Benzedrine, Dexedrine, Ritalin, Preludin, Methamphetamine, Speed, Ice, Crystal
Cannabis:	Marijuana, Hashish
Hallucinogens:	LSD (Acid), Mescaline, Mushrooms (Psilocybin), Peyote, Green, PCP (Phencyclidine), Angel Dust, Ecstasy
Inhalants:	Nitrous Oxide, Amyl Nitrate (Whippits, Poppers), Glue, Solvents, Gasoline, Toluene, Etc.
Just note if these are used:	Antidepressants Ulcer Meds = Zantac, Tagamet Asthma Meds = Ventoline Inhaler, Theodur Other Meds = Antipsychotics, Lithium

ALCOHOL/DRUG USE INSTRUCTIONS:

The following questions refer to two time periods: the past 30 days and lifetime. Lifetime refers to the time prior to the last 30 days.

- 30 day questions only require the number of days used.
- Lifetime use is asked to determine extended periods of use.
- Regular use = 3+ times per week, binges, or problematic irregular use in which normal activities are compromised.
- Alcohol to intoxication does not necessarily mean "drunk", use the words "to feel or felt the effects", "got a buzz", "high", etc., instead of intoxication. As a rule of thumb, 3+ drinks in one sitting, or 5+ drinks in one day defines "intoxication".
- How to ask these questions:

   "How many days in the past 30 have you used...?"

   "How many years in your life have you regularly used...?"

• • •

GENERAL INFORMATION

G1. ID No.:

G2. SS No.:

G4. Date of Admission: /   /

G5. Date of Interview: /   /

G6. Time Begun: (Hour: Minutes)   :

G7. Time Ended: (Hour: Minutes)   :

G8. Class: 1. Intake   2. Follow-up

G9. Contact Code: 1. In person

   2. Telephone (Intake ASI must be in person)

G10. Gender: 1. Male 2. Female

G99. Treatment Episode No.:

G11. Interviewer Code No./ Initials:

G12. Special: 1. Patient terminated

   2. Patient refused

   3. Patient unable to respond

Name
Address 1
Address 2
City State Zip Code

G14. How long have you lived
at this address? (Years/Months) ☐☐ / ☐☐

G15. Is this address owned by you
or your family? 0-No 1-Yes ☐

G16. Date of birth: (Month/Day/Year) ☐☐ / ☐☐ / ☐☐

G17. Of what race do you consider yourself? ☐

1. White (not Hisp)	5. Asian/Pacific	9. Unknown
2. Black (not Hisp)	6. Hispanic-Mexican	
3. American Indian	7. Hispanic-Puerto Rican	
4. Alaskan Native	8. Hispanic-Cuban	

G18. Do you have a religious preference? ☐

1. Protestant	3. Jewish	5. Other
2. Catholic	4. Islamic	6. None

G19. Have you been in a controlled environment
in the past 30 days? ☐

1. No	4. Medical Treatment
2. Jail	5. Psychiatric Treatment
3. Alcohol/Drug Treat.	6. Other: _____

• A place, theoretically, without access to drugs/alcohol.

G20. How many days? ☐☐

• "NN" if Question G19 is No.
Refers to total number of days detained in the past 30 days.

ADDITIONAL TEST RESULTS

SEVERITY PROFILE

PROBLEMS	0	1	2	3	4	5	6	7	8	9
MEDICAL										
EMP/SUP										
ALCOHOL										
DRUGS										
LEGAL										
FAM/SOC										
PSYCH										

GENERAL INFORMATION COMMENTS
(Include the question number with your notes)

MEDICAL STATUS

M1. *How many times in your life have you been hospitalized for medical problems?

- Include O.D.'s and D.T.'s. Exclude detox, alcohol/drug, psychiatric treatment and childbirth (if no complications). Enter the number of **overnight** hospitalizations for medical problems.

M2. How long ago was your last hospitalization for a physical problem?   Yrs/Mos

- If no hospitalizations in Question M1, then this should be "NN".

M3. Do you have any chronic medical problems which continue to interfere with your life?   0-No 1-Yes

- *If "Yes", specify in comments.*
- A chronic medical condition is a serious physical condition that requires regular care (i.e., medication, dietary restriction) preventing full advantage of their abilities.

M99. **<OPTIONAL>** Number of months pregnant: Mos

- "N" for males, "0" for not pregnant.

M4. Are you taking any prescribed medication on a regular basis for a physical problem?   0-No 1-Yes

- *If Yes, specify in comments.*
- Medication prescribed by a MD for medical conditions; **not psychiatric medicines.** Include medicines prescribed whether or not the patient is currently taking them. The intent is to verify chronic medical problems.

M5. Do you receive a pension for a physical disability?   0-No 1-Yes

- *If Yes, specify in comments.*
- Include Workers' compensation, exclude psychiatric disability.

M6. How many days have you experienced medical problems in the past 30 days?

- Include flu, colds, etc. Include serious ailments related to drugs/alcohol, which would continue even if the patient were abstinent (e.g., cirrhosis of liver, abscesses from needles, etc.).

For Questions M7 & M8, ask the patient to use the Patient Rating scale.

(M7.) How troubled or bothered have you been
by these medical problems in the past 30 days? ☐
- Restrict response to problem days of Question M6.

(M8.) How important to you now is treatment for
these medical problems? ☐
- If client is currently receiving medical treatment, refer to
the need for *additional* medical treatment by the patient.

INTERVIEWER SEVERITY RATING

M9. How would you rate the patient's need for
medical treatment? ☐
- Refers to the patient's need for *additional* medical treatment.

CONFIDENCE RATINGS

Is the above information significantly distorted by:

(M10.) Patient's misrepresentation? 0-No 1-Yes ☐

(M11.) Patient's inability to understand? 0-No 1-Yes ☐

MEDICAL COMMENTS
(Include the question number with your notes)

_____

_____

_____

_____

_____

_____

_____

_____

EMPLOYMENT/SUPPORT STATUS

E1. *Education completed: Yrs/Mos ☐☐ / ☐☐
- GED = 12 years, note in comments.
- Include formal education only.

E2. *Training or Technical education completed: Mos ☐☐
- Formal/organized training only. For military training, only include training that can be used in civilian life (i.e., electronics, artillery).

E3. Do you have a profession, trade, or skill? 0-No 1-Yes ☐
- Employable, transferable skill acquired through training.
- If "Yes" (specify) _____

E4. Do you have a valid driver's license? 0-No 1-Yes ☐
- Valid license; not suspended/revoked.

E5. Do you have an automobile available? 0-No 1-Yes ☐
- If answer to E4 is "No", then E5 must be "No". Does not require ownership, only requires availability on a regular basis.

E6. How long was your longest full-time job? Yrs/Mos ☐☐ / ☐☐
- Full-time = 35+ hours weekly; does not necessarily mean most recent job.

E7. *Usual (or last) occupation? (specify) _____ ☐
(use Hollingshead Categories Reference Sheet)

E8. Does someone contribute to your support in any way? 0-No 1-Yes ☐
- Is patient receiving any regular support (i.e., cash, food, housing) from family/friend? Include spouse's contribution; exclude support by an institution.

continued

139

continued

E9. Does this constitute the majority
of your support?

0-No 1-Yes

• If E8 is "No", then E9 is "N".

E10. Usual employment pattern, past three years?

1. Full time (35+ hours)
2. Part time (regular hours)
3. Part time (irregular hours)
4. Student
5. Service
6. Retired/Disability
7. Unemployed
8. In controlled environment

• Answer should represent the majority of the last 3 years,
not just the most recent selection. If there are equal times
for more than one category, select that which best represents
the current situation.

E11. How many days were you paid for working
in the past 30 days?

• Include "under the table" work, paid sick days and vacation.

**For questions E12–E17: How much money did you receive
from the following sources in the past 30 days?**

E12. Employment?

• Net or "take home" pay, include any "under the table" money.

E13. Unemployment Compensation?

E14. Welfare?

• Include food stamps, transportation money provided
by an agency to go to and from treatment.

E15. Pensions, benefits or Social Security?

• Include disability, pensions, retirement, veteran's
benefits, SSI & workers' compensation.

E16. Mate, family, or friends?

• Money for personal expenses (i.e., clothing), include
unreliable sources of income. Record *cash* payments
only, include windfalls (unexpected), money from loans,
legal gambling, inheritance, tax returns, etc.

E17. Illegal?

• *Cash* obtained from drug dealing, stealing, fencing
stolen goods, illegal gambling, prostitution, etc. *Do not*
attempt to convert drugs exchanged to a dollar value.

E18. How many people depend on you for the majority of their food, shelter, etc.?

⬜⬜

• Must be regularly depending on patient, do include alimony/child support, do not include the patient or self-supporting spouse, etc.

E19. How many days have you experienced employment problems in the past 30?

⬜⬜

• Include inability to find work, if they are actively looking for work, or problems with present job in which that job is jeopardized.

For Questions E20 & E21, ask the patient to use the Patient Rating scale.

E20. How troubled or bothered have you been by these employment problems in the past 30 days?

⬜

• If the patient has been incarcerated or detained during the past 30 days, they cannot have employment problems.
In that case an "N" response is indicated.

E21. How important to you now is counseling for these employment problems?

⬜

• Stress help in finding or preparing for a job, not giving them a job.

INTERVIEWER SEVERITY RATING

E22. How would you rate the patient's need for employment counseling?

⬜

CONFIDENCE RATINGS

Is the above information significantly distorted by:

E23. Patient's misrepresentation?   0-No 1-Yes ⬜

E24. Patient's inability to understand?   0-No 1-Yes ⬜

Addiction Severity Index, Fifth Edition

```
┌─────────────────────────────────────────────────┐
│         EMPLOYMENT/SUPPORT COMMENTS               │
│      (Include the question number with your notes)│
│  _____  │
│  _____  │
│  _____  │
│  _____  │
│  _____  │
│  _____  │
└─────────────────────────────────────────────────┘
```

ALCOHOL/DRUGS

```
┌───────────────────────────────────────────────────────────┐
│              Route of Administration Types:                 │
│   1. Oral   2. Nasal   3. Smoking   4. Non-IV injection  5. IV│
│  *Note the usual or most recent route. For more than one route,│
│   choose the most severe. The routes are listed from least    │
│   severe to most severe.                                      │
│                                    Past 30 Days  Lifetime  Route of│
│                                                  (years)   Admin  │
│  D1.  Alcohol (any use at all)       [  ][  ]   [  ][  ]    ■    │
│  D2.  Alcohol (to intoxication)      [  ][  ]   [  ][  ]    ■    │
│  D3.  Heroin                         [  ][  ]   [  ][  ]   [  ]  │
│  D4.  Methadone                      [  ][  ]   [  ][  ]   [  ]  │
│  D5.  Other Opiates/Analgesics       [  ][  ]   [  ][  ]   [  ]  │
│  D6.  Barbiturates                   [  ][  ]   [  ][  ]   [  ]  │
│  D7.  Sedatives/Hypnotics/Tranquilizers [ ][ ]  [  ][  ]   [  ]  │
│  D8.  Cocaine                        [  ][  ]   [  ][  ]   [  ]  │
│  D9.  Amphetamines                   [  ][  ]   [  ][  ]   [  ]  │
│  D10. Cannabis                       [  ][  ]   [  ][  ]   [  ]  │
│  D11. Hallucinogens                  [  ][  ]   [  ][  ]   [  ]  │
│  D12. Inhalants                      [  ][  ]   [  ][  ]   [  ]  │
│  D13. More than 1 substance          [  ][  ]   [  ][  ]    ■    │
│       per day (including alcohol)                             │
└───────────────────────────────────────────────────────────┘
```

D14. According to the interviewer, which substance(s) is/are the major problem?

• Interviewer should determine the major drug of abuse. Code the number next to the drug in questions 01–12, or "00" = no problem, "15" = alcohol & one or more drugs, "16" = more than one drug but no alcohol. Ask patient when not clear.

D98. <OPTIONAL> According to the patient, which substance is the major problem?

D15. How long was your last period of voluntary abstinence from this major substance? Mos

• Last attempt of at least one month, not necessarily the longest. Periods of hospitalization/incarceration *do not count.* Periods of antabuse, methadone, or naltrexone use during abstinence *do count.*

D16. How many months ago did this abstinence end?

• If D15 = "00", then D16 = "NN".
• "00" = still abstinent.

D17. *How many times have you had: Alcohol DT's?

• *Delirium Tremens* (DT's): Occur 24–48 hours after last drink, or significant decrease in alcohol intake, shaking, severe disorientation, fever, hallucinations, they usually require medical attention.

D18. *Overdosed on Drugs?

• *Overdoses* (OD): Requires intervention by someone to recover, not simply sleeping it off, include suicide attempts by OD.

How many times in your life have you been treated for:

D19. *Alcohol abuse?

D20. *Drug abuse?

• Include detoxification, halfway houses, in/outpatient counseling, and AA or NA (if 3+ meetings within one month period).

continued

continued

How many of these were detox only:

(D21.) *Alcohol?

(D22.) *Drugs?

- If D19 = "00," then question D21 is "NN"
- If D20 = "00," then question D22 is "NN"

How much money would you say you spent during the past 30 days on:

(D23.) Alcohol?

(D24.) Drugs?

- Only count actual *money* spent. What is the financial burden caused by drugs/alcohol?

(D25.) How many days have you been treated in an outpatient setting for alcohol or drugs in the past 30 days?

- Include AA/NA

(D99.) <OPTIONAL> How many days have you been treated in an inpatient setting for alcohol or drugs in the past 30 days?

How many days in the past 30 have you experienced:

(D26.) Alcohol problems?

(D27.) Drug problems?

- Include: Craving, withdrawal symptoms, disturbing effects of use, or wanting to stop and being unable to.

For Questions D28–D31, ask the patient to use the Patient Rating scale. The patient is rating the need for additional substance abuse treatment.

How troubled or bothered have you been in the past 30 days by these:

(D28.) Alcohol problems? ☐

(D29.) Drug problems? ☐

How important to you now is treatment for these:

(D30.) Alcohol problems? ☐

(D31.) Drug problems? ☐

INTERVIEWER SEVERITY RATING

How would you rate the patient's need for treatment for

D32. Alcohol problems? ☐

D33. Drug problems? ☐

CONFIDENCE RATINGS
Is the above information significantly distorted by:

(D34.) Patient's misrepresentation?   0-No 1-Yes ☐

(D35.) Patient's inability to understand?   0-No 1-Yes ☐

ALCOHOL/DRUGS COMMENTS
(Include the question number with your notes)

_____

_____

_____

_____

_____

LEGAL STATUS

L1. Was this admission prompted or suggested
by the criminal justice system? 0-No 1-Yes ☐
  • Judge, probation/parole officer, etc.

L2. Are you on parole or probation? 0-No 1-Yes ☐
  • Note duration and level in comments.

**How many times in your life have you been arrested
and charged with the following:**

L3. *Shoplift/Vandal ☐☐	L10. *Assault	☐☐
L4. *Parole/Probation Violations ☐☐	L11. *Arson	☐☐
L5. *Drug Charges ☐☐	L12. *Rape	☐☐
L6. *Forgery ☐☐	L13. *Homicide/Mansl.	☐☐
L7. *Weapons Offense ☐☐	L14. *Prostitution	☐☐
L8. *Burglary/Larceny/ B&E ☐☐	L15. *Contempt of Court	☐☐
L9. *Robbery ☐☐	L16. *Other: _____	☐☐

  • Include total number of counts, not just convictions. Do not include juvenile
    (pre-age 18) crimes, unless they were charged as an adult.
  • Include formal charges only.

L17. How many of these charges resulted in convictions? ☐☐
  • If L3–16 = 00, then question L17 = "NN".
  • Do not include misdemeanor offenses from questions L18–20 below.
  • Convictions include fines, probation, incarcerations, suspended
    sentences, guilty pleas, and plea bargaining.

How many times in your life have you been charged
with the following:

L18. *Disorderly conduct, vagrancy, public intoxication? ☐☐

L19. *Driving while intoxicated? ☐☐

L20. *Major driving violations? ☐☐
- Moving violations: speeding, reckless driving, no license, etc.

L21. *How many months were you incarcerated
in your life? ☐☐
- If incarcerated 2 weeks or more, round this up to 1 month.
  List total number of months incarcerated.

L22. How long was your *last* incarceration? Mos ☐☐
- Enter "NN" if never incarcerated.

L23. What was it for? ☐☐
- Use code 03–16, 18–20. If multiple charges, choose
  most severe. Enter "NN" if never incarcerated.

L24. Are you presently awaiting charges, trial
or sentence? 0-No 1-Yes ☐

L25. What for? ☐☐
- Use the number of the type of crime committed: 03–16 and 18–20.
- Refers to Q. L24. If more than one, choose most severe.

L26. How many days in the past 30, were you
detained or incarcerated? ☐☐
- Include being arrested and released on the same day.

L27. How many days in the past 30 have you engaged
in illegal activities for profit? ☐☐
- Exclude simple drug possession. Include drug dealing,
  prostitution, selling stolen goods, etc. May be cross checked
  with Question E17 under Employment/Family Support Section.

For Questions L28–L29, ask the patient to use the Patient Rating scale.

L28. How serious do you feel your present
legal problems are?

• Exclude civil problems.

L29. How important to you now is counseling
or referral for these legal problems?

• Patient is rating a need for *additional* referral to legal counsel
for defense against criminal charges.

INTERVIEWER SEVERITY RATING

L30. How would you rate the patient's need for
legal services or counseling?

CONFIDENCE RATINGS

Is the above information significantly distorted by:

L31. Patient's misrepresentation?   0-No 1-Yes

L32. Patient's inability to understand?   0-No 1-Yes

LEGAL COMMENTS

(Include the question number with your notes)

_____

_____

_____

_____

_____

FAMILY HISTORY

Have any of your blood-related relatives had what you would call a significant drinking, drug use, or psychiatric problem? Specifically, was there a problem that did or should have led to treatment?

Mother's Side	Alcohol	Drug	Psych.
H1. Grandmother	☐	☐	☐
H2. Grandfather	☐	☐	☐
H3. Mother	☐	☐	☐
H4. Aunt	☐	☐	☐
H5. Uncle	☐	☐	☐

Father's Side	Alcohol	Drug	Psych.
H6. Grandmother	☐	☐	☐
H7. Grandfather	☐	☐	☐
H8. Father	☐	☐	☐
H9. Aunt	☐	☐	☐
H10. Uncle	☐	☐	☐

Siblings	Alcohol	Drug	Psych.
H11. Brother	☐	☐	☐
H12. Sister	☐	☐	☐

0 = Clearly No for any relatives in that category

1 = Clearly Yes for any relatives in that category

X = Uncertain or don't know

N = Never was a relative

• In cases where there is more than one person for a category, report the most severe. Accept the patient's judgment on these questions.

```
┌─────────────────────────────────────────────────────────────┐
│                  FAMILY HISTORY COMMENTS                      │
│  _____  │
│  _____  │
│  _____  │
│  _____  │
│  _____  │
└─────────────────────────────────────────────────────────────┘
```

FAMILY/SOCIAL RELATIONSHIPS

F1. Marital Status: ☐

1. Married	3. Widowed	5. Divorced
2. Remarried	4. Separated	6. Never Married

• Common-law marriage = 1. Specify in comments.

F2. How long have you been in this marital status (Q #F1)? Yrs/Mos ☐☐ / ☐☐

• If never married, then since age 18.

F3. Are you satisfied with this situation? 0-No 1-Indifferent 2-Yes ☐

• Satisfied = generally liking the situation.
• Refers to Questions F1 & F2.

F4. *Usual living arrangements (past 3 years): ☐

1. With sexual partner & children	6. With friends
2. With sexual partner alone	7. Alone
3. With children alone	8. Controlled Environment
4. With parents	9. No stable arrangement
5. With family	

• Choose arrangements most representative of the past 3 years. If there is an even split in time between these arrangements, choose the most recent arrangement.

F5. How long have you lived in these arrangements? Yrs/Mos ☐☐ / ☐☐

• If with parents or family, since age 18.
• Code years and months living in arrangements from Question F4.

F6. Are you satisfied with these arrangements? 0-No 1-Indifferent 2-Yes ☐

Do you live with anyone who:

F7. Has a current alcohol problem? 0-No 1-Yes ☐

F8. Uses non-prescribed drugs? (or abuses prescribed drugs) 0-No 1-Yes ☐

F9. With whom do you spend most of your free time? ☐

    1. Family   2. Friends   3. Alone

    • If a girlfriend/boyfriend is considered as family by patient, then they must refer to them as family throughout this section, not a friend.

F10. Are you satisfied with spending your free time this way? 0-No 1-Indifferent 2-Yes ☐

    • A satisfied response must indicate that the person generally likes the situation. Referring to Question F9.

F11. How many close friends do you have? ☐

    • Stress that you mean *close*. Exclude family members. These are "reciprocal" relationships or mutually supportive relationships.

Would you say you have had a close reciprocal relationship with any of the following people:

F12. Mother ☐

F13. Father ☐

F14. Brothers/Sisters ☐

F15. Sexual Partner/ Spouse ☐

F16. Children ☐

F17. Friends ☐

    0 = Clearly No for all in class
    1 = Clearly Yes for any in class
    X = Uncertain or "I don't know"
    N = Never was a relative

    • By reciprocal, you mean "that you would do anything you could to help them out and vice versa".

Have you had significant periods in which you have experienced serious problems getting along with:

	0-No Past 30 Days	1-Yes In Your Life
(F18.) Mother	☐	☐
(F19.) Father	☐	☐
(F20.) Brother/Sister	☐	☐
(F21.) Sexual Partner/Spouse	☐	☐
(F22.) Children	☐	☐
(F23.) Other Significant Family (specify)_____	☐	☐
(F24.) Close Friends	☐	☐
(F25.) Neighbors	☐	☐
(F26.) Co-workers	☐	☐

• "Serious problems" mean those that endangered the relationship.
• A "problem" requires contact of some sort, either by telephone or in person.

Has anyone ever abused you?

	0-No Past 30 Days	1-Yes In Your Life
F27. Emotionally? • Made you feel bad through harsh words.	☐	☐
F28. Physically? • Caused you physical harm.	☐	☐
F29. Sexually? • Forced sexual advances/acts.	☐	☐

How many days in the past 30 have you had serious conflicts:

F30. With your family? ☐☐

F31. With other people (excluding family)? ☐☐

For Questions F32–35, ask the patient to use the Patient Rating scale.

How troubled or bothered have you been in the past 30 days by:

(F32.) Family problems? ☐

(F33.) Social problems? ☐

How important to you now is treatment or counseling for these:

(F34.) Family problems ☐
  • Patient is rating his/her need for counseling for family problems,
    not whether they would be willing to attend.

(F35.) Social problems ☐
  • Include patient's need to seek treatment for such social problems
    as loneliness, inability to socialize, and dissatisfaction with friends.
    Patient rating should refer to dissatisfaction, conflicts, or other
    serious problems.

INTERVIEWER SEVERITY RATING

F36. How would you rate the patient's need for
family and/or social counseling? ☐

CONFIDENCE RATINGS

Is the above information significantly distorted by:

(F37.) Patient's misrepresentation? 0-No 1-Yes ☐

(F38.) Patient's inability to understand? 0-No 1-Yes ☐

FAMILY/SOCIAL COMMENTS
(Include the question number with your notes)

_____

_____

_____

_____

PSYCHIATRIC STATUS

How many times have you been treated for any psychological or emotional problems:

(P1.) *In a hospital or inpatient setting?

(P2.) *Outpatient/private patient?

> • Do not include substance abuse, employment, or family counseling. Treatment episode = a series of more or less continuous visits or treatment days, not the number of visits or treatment days.
> • Enter diagnosis in comments if known.

(P3.) Do you receive a pension for a psychiatric disability?

0-No 1-Yes

Have you had a significant period of time (that was not a direct result of alcohol/drug use) in which you have:

	0-No	1-Yes
	Past 30 Days	Lifetime

(P4.) Experienced serious depression-sadness, hopelessness, loss of interest, difficulty with daily function?

(P5.) Experienced serious anxiety/tension-uptight, unreasonably worried, inability to feel relaxed?

(P6.) Experienced hallucinations-saw things/heard voices that others didn't see/hear?

(P7.) Experienced trouble understanding, concentrating, or remembering?

(P8.) Experienced trouble controlling violent behavior including episodes of rage, or violence?

> • Patient can be under the influence of alcohol/drugs.

continued

continued

	0-No	1-Yes
	Past 30 Days	Lifetime

P9. Experienced serious thoughts of suicide? □ □

　• Patient seriously considered a plan for taking
　　his/her life. Patient can be under the influence
　　of alcohol/drugs.

P10. Attempted suicide? □ □

　• Include actual suicidal gestures or attempts.
　• Patient can be under the influence of alcohol/drugs.

P11. Been prescribed medication for any
psychological or emotional problems? □ □

　• Prescribed for the patient by a physician.
　　Record "Yes" if a medication was prescribed
　　even if the patient is not taking it.

P12. How many days in the past 30 have you
experienced these psychological or
emotional problems? □□

　• This refers to problems noted in Questions P4–P10.

For Questions P13–P14, ask the patient to use the Patient Rating scale.

P13. How much have you been troubled or bothered
by these psychological or emotional problems
in the past 30 days? □

　• Patient should be rating the problem days from Question P12.

P14. How important to you now is treatment for
these psychological or emotional problems? □

The following items are to be completed by the interviewer.

At the time of the interview, the patient was   0-No 1-Yes

(P15.) Obviously depressed/withdrawn ☐

(P16.) Obviously hostile ☐

(P17.) Obviously anxious/nervous ☐

(P18.) Having trouble with reality testing, thought
disorders, paranoid thinking ☐

(P19.) Having trouble comprehending,
concentrating, remembering ☐

(P20.) Having suicidal thoughts ☐

INTERVIEWER SEVERITY RATING

P21. How would you rate the patient's need for
psychiatric/psychological treatment? ☐

CONFIDENCE RATINGS

Is the above information significantly distorted by:

(P22.) Patient's misrepresentation?   0-No 1-Yes ☐

(P23.) Patient's inability to understand?   0-No 1-Yes ☐

PSYCHIATRIC STATUS COMMENTS
(Include the question number with your notes)

_____

_____

_____

_____

Source: A. T. McLellan et al.,"The Fifth Edition of the Addiction Severity Index," *Journal of Substance Abuse Treatment* 9 (1992): 199–213.

Form 90

Form 90-AQ: Quick Drinking Assessment Interview

"I'd like to ask you just six questions about your drinking during the period from _____ up through yesterday. That's a period of _____ days."

"First of all, on how many days during this period did you have at least one drink containing alcohol?"

(Record as item 5a.)

(To confirm the answer to item 5a:)

"So that means there were (item 2 minus item 5) days during this period when you didn't drink at all."

(Confirm and record below.)
(Item 5a + item 5b must = item 2.)

"Now on those days when you did drink, how much did you have to drink on average?"

(Probe and record as nearest whole number of standard drink units* for item 6.)

"Now on those (read number from item 5a) days on which you drank, on how many did you have six or more drinks?"

(Record as item 7.)

"When was the first day that you had a drink during this period?"

(Record as item 8.)

1. For period from
   _____/_____/_____
   through
   _____/_____/_____

2. Number of days in this assessment period: _____

3. This is a _____ month follow-up

4. Interview conducted:
   _____ (1) on site
   _____ (2) by telephone
   _____ (3) home visit
   _____ (4) other location

5a. Total number of drinking days during period: _____

5b. Total number of abstinent days during period: _____

6. Number of standard drinks per day:
   _____

7. Total number of heavy drinking days per period: _____

8. Date of first drink during period:
   _____/_____/_____

continued

"And when was the first day that you had six or more drinks in the same day?"

(Record date as item 9.)

"And when did you have your last drink?"

(Record date as item 10.)

(If appropriate, continue with longer interview such as Form 90-AT.)

* Standard drink unit =
  1 glass of wine (4 oz.) =
  1 can of beer (10 oz.) =
  1 hard drink (1/4 oz. of 80 proof liquor)

9. Date of first heavy drinking day in period:

   ____/____/____

10. Date of last drink during period:

    ____/____/____

Form 90

Form 90-AF: Follow-up Interview Assessment
of Drinking and Related Behaviors

Other Drug Use

"Now I'm going to show you this set of cards, which you have seen before. Each card names a kind of drug that people sometimes use. I'd like you to sort them into two piles for me. In one pile here (indicate position and use marker card), I'd like you to place those cards that name a kind of drug that you have used at least once during this period. In the other pile here (indicate position and use marker card), place the cards that name types of drugs that you have not used at all, not even once, during this period."

Give cards to client in numerical order, with nicotine on top, cannabis next, and so on. When the sorting has been completed, take the NO pile and mark all these categories as zero (0) days on items 48–58, respectively. Then for each of the YES cards, ask about specific drug(s) and route(s) of administration. For example:

"Which drug(s) from this group have you used at least once during this period? And how did you take it?

(Routes of administration include oral ingestion, smoke, nasal inhalation, and needle injection.)

(Record on items 48–58.)

(Also determine frequency of use for each drug class:)

"During this period, on how many days would you say you used _____ ?"

(Record on items 48–58 and repeat for all YES cards.)

(If the reported use in a drug category qualifies, enter the number of days of use for that category on the drug use chart. If the reported use does not qualify (e.g., prescribed use for less than 30 days), enter zero (0) days even though the client initially placed the card in the YES pile.)

Form 90

Form 90-AF: Current Drug Use

	Days*
Nicotine Specify number of cigarettes per day in current period: _____	48. _____
Cannabis Specify:	49. _____
Sedatives Specify:	50. _____
Hypnotics Specify:	51. _____
Steroids Specify:	52. _____
Amphetamines Specify:	53. _____
Cocaine Specify:	54. _____
Hallucinogens Specify:	55. _____
Inhaled Toxicants Specify:	56. _____
Opiates Specify:	57. _____
Other Drugs Specify:	58. _____

* Days = Total number of days in which any drug from the class was used during this follow-up window. Do not include drugs used during prior follow-up windows but not this window. Do not report drug use that does not qualify.

Form 90
Drug Card Sort

Copy this sheet onto card stock and cut out cards

Form 90 **Drug Card Sort**	**OTHER DRUGS** Designer Drugs Amyl/Butyl Nitrates (poppers) Nitrous Oxide (laughing gas) Over-the-counter remedies like Dextromethorphan (DM), etc. 11
YES **Drugs I have used at least once**	NO **Drugs I have not used**
NICOTINE Tobacco cigarettes Snuff (dip) Chewing tobacco Nicotine patch or gum 1	**CANNABIS** Marijuana (pot) Hashish 2
SEDATIVES Librium, Valium Ativan, Serax Xanax, etc. 3	**HYPNOTICS (Downers)** Quaalude (ludes) Barbiturates Seconal (reds) Amytal (blues) Nembutal (yellow jackets), etc. 4

Copy this sheet onto card stock and cut out cards

STEROIDS	AMPHETAMINES (Uppers)
	Amphetamine (Speed)
	Methamphetamine
	Dexedrine, Benzedrine
	Ritalin, Ice, etc.
5	6

COCAINE	HALLUCINOGENS
Freebase	LSD (Acid)
Crack	Mescaline (Peyote)
Powder	PCP (Angel Dust)
Paste, etc.	Morning Glory Seeds
	MDMA (Ecstasy)
7	8 Mushrooms, etc.

INHALED TOXICANTS	OPIATES (Downers)
Aerosol Sprays	Heroin, Morphine
Glue	Opium, Methadone
Paint	Percodan, Demerol
Gasoline, etc.	Codeine, etc.
9	10

Use the following card for Form 90-D only.

ALCOHOL
Beer, Wine
Liquor, etc.
0

Source: W. R. Miller, *Form 90: A Structured Assessment Interview for Drinking and Related Behaviors.* (Bethesda, Md: National Institute on Alcohol Abuse and Alcoholism, 1996). See also *www.niaaa.nih.gov/publications/match.htm.*

Assessment for Warning Signs for Relapse

		NEVER	SOMETIMES	OFTEN	ALWAYS
1.	I feel nervous or unsure of my ability to stay sober	1—2—3—4—5—6—7			
2.	I have many problems in my life	1—2—3—4—5—6—7			
3.	I tend to overreact or act impulsively	1—2—3—4—5—6—7			
4.	I keep to myself and feel lonely	1—2—3—4—5—6—7			
5.	I get too focused on one area of my life	1—2—3—4—5—6—7			
6.	I feel blue, down, listless, or depressed	1—2—3—4—5—6—7			
7.	I engage in wishful thinking	1—2—3—4—5—6—7			
8.	The plans that I make succeed*	1—2—3—4—5—6—7			
9.	I have trouble concentrating, and prefer to dream about how things could be	1—2—3—4—5—6—7			
10.	Things don't work out well for me	1—2—3—4—5—6—7			
11.	I feel confused	1—2—3—4—5—6—7			
12.	I get irritated or annoyed with my friends	1—2—3—4—5—6—7			
13.	I feel angry or frustrated	1—2—3—4—5—6—7			
14.	I have good eating habits*	1—2—3—4—5—6—7			
15.	I feel trapped and stuck, like there is no way out	1—2—3—4—5—6—7			
16.	I have trouble sleeping	1—2—3—4—5—6—7			
17.	I have long periods of serious depression	1—2—3—4—5—6—7			

continued on next page

	NEVER	SOMETIMES	OFTEN	ALWAYS
18. I don't really care what happens	1—2—3—4—5—6—7
19. I feel like things are so bad that I might as well drink	1—2—3—4—5—6—7
20. I am able to think clearly*	1—2—3—4—5—6—7
21. I feel sorry for myself	1—2—3—4—5—6—7
22. I think about drinking	1—2—3—4—5—6—7
23. I lie to other people	1—2—3—4—5—6—7
24. I feel hopeful and confident*	1—2—3—4—5—6—7
25. I feel angry at the world in general	1—2—3—4—5—6—7
26. I am doing things to stay sober	1—2—3—4—5—6—7
27. I am afraid I am losing my mind	1—2—3—4—5—6—7
28. I am drinking out of control	1—2—3—4—5—6—7

*Reversed scale

Source: W. R. Miller and R. J. Harris, "Simple Scale of Gorski's Warning Signs for Relapse," *Journal of Studies on Alcohol* 61 (2000): 759–65.

CES-D

Below is a list of some of the ways you may have felt or behaved. Please indicate how often you have felt this way during the past week by checking ✔ the appropriate space.

	During the past week:	Rarely or none of the time (less than 1 day)	Some or a little of the time (1–2 days)	Occasionally or a moderate amount of time (3–4 days)	Most or all of the time (5–7 days)
1.	I was bothered by things that usually don't bother me.				
2.	I did not feel like eating; my appetite was poor.				
3.	I felt that I could not shake off the blues even with help from my family or friends.				
4.	I felt that I was just as good as other people.				
5.	I had trouble keeping my mind on what I was doing.				
6.	I felt depressed.				
7.	I felt that everything I did was an effort.				
8.	I felt hopeful about the future.				
9.	I thought my life had been a failure.				
10.	I felt fearful.				
11.	My sleep was restless.				
12.	I was happy.				
13.	I talked less than usual.				
14.	I felt lonely.				
15.	People were unfriendly.				
16.	I enjoyed life.				
17.	I had crying spells.				

continued

	During the past week:	Rarely or none of the time (less than 1 day)	Some or a little of the time (1–2 days)	Occasionally or a moderate amount of time (3–4 days)	Most or all of the time (5–7 days)
18.	I felt sad.				
19.	I felt that people disliked me.				
20.	I could not get going.				

Source: L. S. Radloff, "The CES-D Scale: A Self-report Depression Scale for Research in the General Population," *Applied Psychological Measurement* 1 (1977): 385–401.

SF-12

1. In general, would you say your health is:

☐ Excellent ☐ Very Good ☐ Good ☐ Fair ☐ Poor

The following items are about activities you might do during a typical day. Does your health now limit you in these activities? If so, how much?

	Yes, limited a lot	Yes, limited a little	No, not limited at all
2. *Moderate* activities, such as moving a table, pushing a vacuum cleaner, bowling or playing golf.	☐	☐	☐
3. *Climbing* several flights of stairs	☐	☐	☐

During the past four weeks, have you had any of the following problems with your work or other regular daily activities as a result of your physical health?

4. Accomplished less than you would like ☐ Yes ☐ No

5. Were limited in the *kind* of work or other activities ☐ Yes ☐ No

During the past four weeks, have you had any of the following problems with your work or other daily activities as a result of emotional problems (such as feeling depressed or anxious)?

6. *Accomplished less* than you would like ☐ Yes ☐ No

7. Didn't do work or other activities *as carefully* as usual. ☐ Yes ☐ No

8. During the past four weeks, how much did pain interfere with your normal work (including both work outside the home and housework)?

☐ Not at all ☐ A little bit ☐ Moderately ☐ Quite a bit ☐ Extremely

continued

These questions are about how you feel and how things have been with you during the past 4 weeks. For each question, please give the one answer that comes closest to the way you have been feeling.

	All of the time	Most of the time	A good bit of the time	Some of the time	A little of the time	None of the time
	1	2	3	4	5	6
9. Have you felt calm & peaceful?	☐	☐	☐	☐	☐	☐
10. Did you have a lot of energy?	☐	☐	☐	☐	☐	☐
11. Have you felt downhearted & blue?	☐	☐	☐	☐	☐	☐

12. During the past four weeks, how much of the time has your physical health or emotional problems interfered with your social activities (like visiting friends, relatives, etc.)?

☐	☐	☐	☐	☐
All of the time	Most of the time	Some of the time	A little of the time	None of the time

Source: J. E. Ware, M. Kosinski, and S. D. Keller, "A 12-Item Short-Form Health Survey (SF-12®): Construction of Scales and Preliminary Tests of Reliability and Validity," *Medical Care* 32 (1996): 220–33.

APPENDIX 7

Items of the Alcoholics Anonymous Involvement (AAI) Scale

Item	Response	
1. Have you ever attended an AA meeting?	☐ No	☐ Yes
2. Have you attended an AA meeting in the last year?	☐ No	☐ Yes
3. Have you ever considered yourself to be a member of AA?	☐ No	☐ Yes
4. Have you ever gone to 90 AA meetings in 90 days?	☐ No	☐ Yes
5. Have you ever celebrated an AA sobriety birthday?	☐ No	☐ Yes
6. Have you ever had an AA sponsor?	☐ No	☐ Yes
7. Have you ever been an AA sponsor?	☐ No	☐ Yes
8. If you have been in an alcohol treatment program (inpatient or outpatient), did they require that you "work" any of the AA Steps?	☐ No	☐ Yes

9. What Steps did you complete when you were in alcohol treatment?

Circle all that apply. 1 2 3 4 5 6 7 8 9 10 11 12

10. *Regardless* of whether you have or have not been to alcohol treatment, which of the 12 Steps of AA have you "worked"?

Circle all that apply. 1 2 3 4 5 6 7 8 9 10 11 12

11. How many AA meetings have you attended in the last year? Please enter your best estimate. If you did not attend any AA meetings in the last year, enter zero (0).

_____

continued

Items of the Alcoholics Anonymous Involvement (AAI) Scale

Item	Response
12. What is the *total* number of AA meetings that you have ever attended? Please enter your best estimate. If you have never attended any meeting, enter zero (0).	_____
13. Have you ever had a spiritual awakening or conversion experience since your involvement in AA?	☐ No ☐ Yes

Source: J. S. Tonigan, G. J. Connors, and W. R. Miller, "Alcoholics Anonymous Involvement (AAI) Scale: Reliability and Norms," *Psychology of Addictive Behaviors* 10 (1996): 75–80.

Alcoholics Anonymous Affiliation Scale

Interviewer: "I would like to ask you some questions about Alcoholics Anonymous (AA)."

1. How many AA meetings would you estimate that you've gone to during your lifetime?

    None (STOP ADMINISTRATION. SCORE TOTAL SCALE AS ZERO.)
    Less than 30
    Between 30 and 90
    Over 90 but less than 500
    Over 500

2. How many AA meetings have you gone to in the last 12 months? _____ (# of Meetings)

3. Have you considered yourself a member of AA?   ☐ No   ☐ Yes

4. Have you ever called an AA member for help?   ☐ No   ☐ Yes

5. Do you *now* have an AA sponsor?   ☐ No   ☐ Yes

6. Have you ever sponsored anyone in AA?   ☐ No   ☐ Yes

7. Have you had a spiritual awakening or a conversion experience as a result of your involvement in AA?   ☐ No   ☐ Yes

8. In the past 12 months, have you read AA literature?   ☐ No   ☐ Yes

9. In the past 12 months, have you done service, helped newcomers, or set up chairs, made coffee, cleaned up after a meeting, etc.?   ☐ No   ☐ Yes

HOW TO SCORE THE SCALE

STEP #1:   On items 1 and 2, score each item 0 for no meetings, .25 for 1 to 30 meetings, .50 for between 30 and 90 meetings, .75 for over 90 but less than 500 meetings, and 1.0 for over 500 meetings.

continued

STEP #2:   For items 3–9, score each item 0 for a no answer and 1 for a yes answer.

STEP #3:   Sum scores for all 9 items to get overall scale score, which can range from 0 to 9.

Source: K. Humphreys, L. A. Kaskutas, and C. Weisner, "Alcoholics Anonymous Affiliation Scale: Development, Reliability, and Norms for Diverse Treated and Untreated Populations," *Alcoholism: Clinical and Experimental Research* 22 (1998): 974–78.

Common Response Categories

1 Strongly Disagree 2 Disagree 3 Neither agree nor disagree 4 Agree 5 Strongly agree	1 Very dissatisfied 2 A little dissatisfied 3 Moderately satisfied 4 Very satisfied
1 Much worse 2 Somewhat worse 3 About the same 4 Somewhat better 5 Much better	1 None of the time 2 Some of the time 3 Most of the time 4 All of the time
1 Much less than I expected 2 Less than I expected 3 About what I expected 4 More than what I expected 5 Much more than I expected	1 Not useful 2 Somewhat useful 3 Very useful
1 Not at all helpful 2 Only slightly helpful 3 Moderately helpful 4 Very helpful	1 Excellent 2 Good 3 Fair 4 Poor

Notes

Chapter Two: Deciding What to Measure

1. R. A. Cisler and A. Zweben, "Development of a Composite Measure for Assessing Alcohol Treatment Outcome: Operationalization and Validity," *Alcoholism: Clinical and Experimental Research* 23 (1999): 263–71.

Chapter Three: Designing the Questionnaire

1. A. T. McLellan et al., "Improved Diagnostic Evaluation Instrument for Substance Abuse Patients: The Addiction Severity Index," *Journal of Nervous and Mental Disease* 168 (1980): 26–33.

2. A. T. McLellan et al., "Fifth Edition of the Addiction Severity Index," *Journal of Substance Abuse Treatment* 9 (1992): 199–213.

3. R. L. Stout, "Project MATCH: Treatment Implications of Long-term Results," *Alcohol and Alcoholism: International Journal of the Medical Council on Alcoholism* 34 (1999): 116.

4. L. C. Sobell et al., "Reliability of the Alcohol Timeline Follow-back When Administered by Telephone and by Computer," *Drug and Alcohol Dependence* 42 (1996): 49–54.

5. American Psychiatric Association, *Diagnostic and Statistical Manual of Mental Disorders*, 4th ed. (Washington, D.C.: American Psychiatric Association, 1994).

6. W. R. Miller and R. J. Harris, "Simple Scale of Gorski's Warning Signs for Relapse," *Journal of Studies on Alcohol* 61 (2000): 759–65.

7. T. T. Gorski, "CENAPS Model of Relapse Prevention Therapy (CMRPT)," in *Approaches to Drug Abuse Counseling*, eds. J. J. Boren, L. S. Onken, and K. M. Carroll (Bethesda, Md.: National Institute on Drug Abuse, 2000).

8. Unpublished Hazelden data.

9. B. Michael et al., *Structured Clinical Interview for DSM-IV Personality Disorders* (SCID-II) (Washington, D.C.: American Psychiatric Press, 1997).

10. BASIS-32 is available by contacting Dr. Susan Eisen, Department of Mental Health Services, McLean Hospital, 115 Mill Street, Belmont, MA 02478. Fax 617-855-2948. See also www.basis-32.org.

11. L. S. Radloff, "The CES-D Scale: A Self-Report Depression Scale for Research in the General Population," *Applied Psychological Measurement* 1 (1977): 385–401. See also www.wpic.pitt.edu/research/City/OnlineScreeningFiles/CesdDescription.htm.

12. See www.psychcorpcenter.com/content/bdi-II.htm.

13. R. A. Chubon, "Developing a Quality of Life Rating Scale for Use in Health Care Evaluation," *Evaluation and the Health Professions* 10 (1987): 186–200.

14. J. H. Foster, E. J. Marshall, and T. J. Peters, "Application of a Quality of Life Measure, the Life Situation Survey (LSS), to Alcohol-Dependent Subjects in Relapse and Remission," *Alcoholism: Clinical and Experimental Research* 24 (2000): 1687–92.

15. J. Ware, M. Kosinski, and S. D. Keller, "A Twelve-Item Short Form Health Survey: Construction of Scales and Preliminary Tests of Reliability and Validity," *Medical Care* 32 (1996): 220–33.

16. K. B. Wells and C. D. Sherbourne, "Functioning and Utility for Depression Compared to Chronic Medical Conditions in Primary Care, Managed Care Patients," *Archives of General Psychiatry* 56 (1999): 897–904.

17. M. D. Stein et al., "Functioning and Well Being of Persons Who Seek Treatment for Drug and Alcohol Use," *Journal of Substance Abuse* 10 (1998): 75–84.

18. F. S. Gilbert, "Development of a 'Steps Questionnaire,'" *Journal of Studies on Alcohol* 52 (1991): 353–60.

19. H. P. Brown, Jr., and J. H. Peterson, Jr., "Assessing Spirituality in Addiction Treatment and Follow-Up: Development of the Brown-Peterson Recovery Progress Inventory (B-PRPI)," *Alcoholism Treatment Quarterly* 8 (1991): 21–50.

20. M. P. Baker, J. D. Sellman, and J. Horn, "Developing a God/Higher Power Scale for Use with Twelve Step Treatment Programs," *Alcoholism Treatment Quarterly* 19 (2001): 45–61.

21. D. F. Reinert, "Surrender Scale: Reliability, Factor Structure, and Validity," *Alcoholism Treatment Quarterly* 15 (1997): 15–32.

22. J. S. Tonigan, G. J. Connors, and W. R. Miller, "Alcoholics Anonymous Involvement (AAI) Scale: Reliability and Norms," *Psychology of Addictive Behaviors* 10 (1996): 75–80.

23. K. Humphreys, L. A. Kaskutas, and C. Weisner, "Alcoholics Anonymous Affiliation Scale: Development, Reliability, and Norms for Diverse Treated and Untreated Populations," *Alcoholism: Clinical and Experimental Research* 22 (1998): 974–78.

24. J. P. Allen, "Measuring Treatment Process Variables in Alcoholics Anonymous," *Journal of Substance Abuse Treatment* 18 (2000): 227–30.

25. P. C. Hill and R. W. Hood, eds., *Measures of Religiosity* (Birmingham, Ala.: Religious Education Press, 1999).

Chapter Four: Implementing the Outcome Study

1. "Outcome Study Guidebook," *A New Direction: A Cognitive Behavioral Treatment Curriculum* (Center City, Minn.: Hazelden, 2002).

2. M. Q. Patton, *Utilization-Focused Evaluation*, 3d ed. (Thousand Oaks, Calif.: Sage Publications, 1997).

Chapter Five: Presenting the Information

1. See www.spss.com.

2. G. J. Connors, J. S. Tonigan, and W. R. Miller, "A Measure of Religious Background and Behavior for Use in Behavior Change Research," *Psychology of Addictive Behaviors* 10 (1996): 90–96.

3. California Department of Alcohol and Drug Programs, *Evaluating Recovery Services: The California Drug and Alcohol Treatment Assessment (CALDATA)* (Sacramento: State of California, July 1994).

Chapter Six: Special Settings and Populations

1. See Butler Center for Research Update on Treatment in Criminal Justice Systems (2002) at www.hazelden.org/research/publication_detail.cfm?id=50.

2. M. L. Dennis et al., "Twenty-five Strategies for Improving the Design, Implementation and Analysis of Health Services Research Related to Alcohol and Other Drug Abuse Treatment," *Addiction* 95 (suppl. 3) (2000): s281–s308. This excellent article provides details about doing research in health maintenance organizations and related systems.

3. B. A. Flannery, J. R. Volpicelli, and H. M. Pettinati, "Psychometric Properties of the Penn Alcohol Craving Scale," *Alcoholism: Clinical and Experimental Research* 23 (1999): 1289–95.

4. R. F. Anton, D. H. Moak, and P. K. Latham, "Obsessive Compulsive Drinking Scale: A New Method of Assessing Outcome in Alcoholism Treatment Studies," *Archives of General Psychiatry* 53 (1996): 225–31.

5. E. S. Lisansky-Gomberg, "Women," in *Addictions: A Comprehensive Guidebook*, eds. B. S. McCrady and E. E. Epstein (New York: Oxford University Press, 1999), 533.

Chapter Seven: Some Landmark Studies

1. G. J. Connors, J. S. Tonigan, and W. R. Miller, "Longitudinal Model of Intake Symptomatology, AA Participation and Outcome: Retrospective Study of the Project MATCH Outpatient and Aftercare Samples," *Journal of Studies on Alcohol* 62 (2001): 817–25.

2. D. M. Donovan, "Efficacy and Effectiveness: Complementary Findings from Two Multisite Trials Evaluating Outcomes of Alcohol Treatments Differing in Theoretical Orientations," *Alcoholism: Clinical and Experimental Research* 23 (1999): 564–72.

3. R. H. Moos et al., "Comparative Evaluation of Substance Abuse Treatment: I. Treatment Orientation, Amount of Care, and 1-Year Outcomes," *Alcoholism: Clinical and Experimental Research* 23 (1999): 529–36.

4. P. C. Ouimette, J. W. Finney, and R. H. Moos, "Twelve-Step and Cognitive-Behavioral Treatment for Substance Abuse: A Comparison of Treatment Effectiveness," *Journal of Consulting and Clinical Psychology* 65 (1997): 230–40.

5. W. R. Miller, S. T. Walters, and M. E. Bennett, "How Effective Is Alcoholism Treatment in the United States?" *Journal of Studies on Alcohol* 62 (2001): 211–20.

6. C. Lowman, J. Allen, and R. L. Stout, "Relapse Research Group Replication and Extension of Marlatt's Taxonomy of Relapse Precipitants: Overview of Procedures and Results," *Addiction* 91 (1996): s51–s71.

7. D. J. Armor, J. M. Polich, and H. B. Stambul, *Alcoholism and Treatment* (New York: John Wiley, 1978).

8. P. A. Harrison and S. E. Asche, "Outcomes Monitoring in Minnesota: Treatment Implications, Practical Limitations," *Journal of Substance Abuse Treatment* 21 (2001): 173–283.

9. A. T. McLellan et al., "Private Substance Abuse Treatments: Are Some Programs More Effective Than Others?" *Journal of Substance Abuse Treatment* 10 (1993): 243–54.

Chapter Eight: New Directions

1. For a review of indicators, see R. A. Cisler and A. Zweben, "Development of a Composite Measure for Assessing Alcohol Treatment Outcome: Operationalization and Validity," *Alcoholism: Clinical and Experimental Research* 23 (1999): 263–71.

2. A. T. McLellan et al., "Drug Dependence, a Chronic Medical Illness: Implications for Treatment, Insurance, and Outcomes Evaluation," *Journal of the American Medical Association* 284 (2000): 1689–95.

3. W. R. Miller, S. T. Walters, and M. E. Bennett, "How Effective Is Alcoholism Treatment in the United States?" *Journal of Studies on Alcohol* 62 (2001): 211–20.

4. A. T. McLellan et al., "Drug Dependence, a Chronic Medical Illness: Implications for Treatment, Insurance, and Outcomes Evaluation," *Journal of the American Medical Association* 284 (2000): 1689–95.

Index

About the Author

Patricia Owen, Ph.D., M.H.A., is executive vice president of Research at Hazelden. She oversees the research arm of Hazelden, with responsibilities for conducting research that improves treatment and recovery at Hazelden, bringing research knowledge into the organization, and helping to advance the field's understanding of addiction. She also directs the Butler Center for Research, a Hazelden leadership initiative dedicated to the advancement of knowledge and understanding of addiction recovery through research, collaboration, and communication.

Owen, a clinical psychologist, has served Hazelden in a number of capacities for more than twenty years. Prior to her current position, she was vice president of Professional and Community Services from 1988 to 1992, manager of Employee Assistance Services from 1986 to 1988, and senior evaluation and unit psychologist from 1980 to 1986. She supervised the quality measurement system for Recovery Services at Hazelden from 1996 to 1999.

In addition, Owen is a clinical assistant professor in the department of psychiatry at the University of Minnesota and has been a lecturer at the College of Saint Catherine in Saint Paul, Minnesota. She is a member of the American Psychological Association.

She holds a bachelor's degree in child psychology (*summa cum laude* and Phi Beta Kappa), a master's degree and doctoral degree in adult clinical psychology, and a master's degree in health administration, all from the University of Minnesota. As a graduate student, she received a National Institute of Mental Health Training Grant and a University of Minnesota Graduate Fellowship. She is a licensed psychologist and has written and presented extensively on a number of subjects related to chemical dependency, including treatment outcomes and the addiction recovery process. She has presented papers and taught workshops nationally and in Ireland, Africa, and Australia. She is the author of *I Can See Tomorrow: A Guide for Living with Depression.* She has appeared as an addiction expert on numerous radio and television shows, including the Bill Moyers PBS series on addiction: *Moyers on Addiction: Close to Home.*

Hazelden Publishing and Educational Services is a division of the Hazelden Foundation, a not-for-profit organization. Since 1949, Hazelden has been a leader in promoting the dignity and treatment of people afflicted with the disease of chemical dependency.

The mission of the foundation is to improve the quality of life for individuals, families, and communities by providing a national continuum of information, education, and recovery services that are widely accessible; to advance the field through research and training; and to improve our quality and effectiveness through continuous improvement and innovation.

Stemming from that, the mission of this division is to provide quality information and support to people wherever they may be in their personal journey—from education and early intervention, through treatment and recovery, to personal and spiritual growth.

Although our treatment programs do not necessarily use everything Hazelden publishes, our bibliotherapeutic materials support our mission and the Twelve Step philosophy upon which it is based. We encourage your comments and feedback.

The headquarters of the Hazelden Foundation are in Center City, Minnesota. Additional treatment facilities are located in Chicago, Illinois; Newberg, Oregon; New York, New York; Plymouth, Minnesota; St. Paul, Minnesota; and West Palm Beach, Florida. At these sites, we provide a continuum of care for men and women of all ages. Our Plymouth facility is designed specifically for youth and families.

For more information on Hazelden,
please call **1-800-257-7800.**

Or you may access our World Wide Web site
on the Internet at **www.hazelden.org.**